THE WIDOW(ER)'S GUIDE
TO RECLAIMING HAPPINESS

HOW TO CREATE YOUR COMEBACK STORY
AFTER LOSS

JEN SANTANIELLO

Edited by Yna Davis

In loving memory of Tim, who showed me what true strength is. I am incredibly grateful for our years together and will forever carry you in my heart.

CONTENTS

IT WASN'T SUPPOSED TO BE THIS WAY

Never in a million years did you expect to become widowed at such a young age. It never even crossed your mind as a possibility, right? Surely the "parting" in "till death do us part" wasn't supposed to come unexpectedly, in the middle of your life, just when you were getting started.

No one, especially not your friends and family who still have their loved ones by their sides, can truly understand what you're feeling in the weeks and months following the loss of your spouse. Even if they've lost relatives of their own, they have no idea what you're going through. How could they? Being young and widowed is not the norm. The best your loved ones can do is imagine what you're going through, and even then, it won't come close to your reality.

Here's what I would tell them: In the beginning, your heart aches in a way it's never hurt before. It longs for what it no longer has as you slowly begin to process what just happened, how this loss will affect the rest of your life, and what your world is going to look like without your spouse in it. Part of you has no words to describe all that you're trying to process internally, so you say nothing. Part of you is half-hoping your spouse will walk through the front door, as if this were all some horrible joke. You can even picture wrapping your arms around their familiar body in relief and never letting go.

And then there's the part of you that keeps asking, *Why?*

Why did this happen? Why me? Why us? Why am I still here?

Your whole world has been unexpectedly upended, and your mind races with questions it can't answer. You start to wonder what kind of god would do this, how it could possibly be real, and if there is a lesson to be learned.

Somehow, you managed to get through the practicalities of losing a loved one, although in a fog. You made funeral arrangements, notified your spouse's employer of their passing, and responded to a myriad of insurance paperwork and legal matters that seemed never-ending. You even canceled services in your spouse's name, closed out credit cards, and terminated policies that were no longer needed. But as you memorialize their social media accounts, closing the curtain on a life that no longer exists, and send out death certificates, watching as your spouse's name becomes seemingly erased from this world, you begin to feel despair on a whole new level. You can't believe they're really gone—and worse, that they're never coming back.

As your friends, family, colleagues, and acquaintances, who were super supportive for so long, start to go back to their own lives, you start to wonder how you will manage your own, *on your own*.

On some level, you know you must move on. After all, life is still moving forward, which astonishes you at times. But you find yourself wondering, *How? How am I supposed to go on?*

What am I supposed to do next? This wasn't the life I planned. What if I can't do this? My poor kids!

Nothing feels the same anymore. Days, weeks, or months ago, you had shared plans and dreams. Now you feel like you're starting all over, and the weight of sudden uncertainty regarding where you go from here or even what to do in the next twenty-four hours feels terrifying. Your whole life—your present and your future—has been altered forever.

Even the day-to-day grind feels overwhelming now that you're a solo parent and the sole provider for your family. Not wanting your kids to suffer any more than they already have, you jump right back into work to ensure that they have everything they ask for and need. You become determined to over-deliver, as if extra toys and activities might compensate for the loss of their other parent. In this sense, your job becomes a means to an end, but it is also a way to keep your mind busy. Loved ones initially encourage you to slow down and take time off to heal, but a pause would have you falling apart at the seams. Work has become an escape and a welcome reprieve from your new reality.

At home, you are an overworked superhero. As soon as you walk through the front door, you begin cooking, cleaning, tidying up, paying bills, and caring for your kids, all by yourself. You barely sit down. You miss the days when you tag-teamed life with a partner, divvying up chores, giving each other sanity breaks, and backing each other up when it came to discipline or handling tantrums. Now that you're on your own, you can't seem to keep up, and you feel defeated when you forget trivial things like taking out the trash. You're in such a constant state of overwhelm that the littlest things tend to set you off, causing you to say and do things that you later regret and making you feel like a terrible parent. Most nights, as you collapse into bed, utterly exhausted, you wonder how you will do it all over again the next day.

To the outside world, you appear to have your act together. You answer "okay" when friends and family ask how you're doing and "fine" when well-meaning members of society ask how your day is going. But, on the inside, you're fighting back tears and screaming, *How could anything be fine?* Behind your well-intentioned facade of strength, you feel broken, shattered even, and scared. Innocent cashiers inquiring about the whereabouts of your spouse threaten to release the floodgates, and happy couples stand out like beacons, symbolizing the life you no longer have. *It isn't fair!* You wonder if life will always feel this hard and if you'll always feel this unhappy.

Nothing feels right with your world anymore, and the waves of grief, which feel more like tsunamis, come and go when you least expect them to, keeping you drowning in despair and anger over the fact that this has happened to you. One minute you're completing tasks at work and engaging easily with colleagues, and the next you're viewing the road home through a sea of tears because a song reminded you of your spouse. One minute you're putting away laundry and getting the kids ready for bed, feeling like you've got a momentary grip on life, and the next, something goes awry, causing anger to well up inside you over the fact that your spouse is not here and you're so tired of managing everything on your own. One minute you're climbing into bed, exhausted by the demands of solo parenting but ready to tell your spouse all about your day—a habit that is unconsciously ingrained in you—and the next, you're full of despair and loneliness when you roll over and face an empty space beside you.

No, nothing compares to losing your best friend and partner in life, and it's hard for others to understand something they haven't experienced themselves. It's why you try so hard to act unphased when your loved ones tell stories—or worse, complain—about their spouses. They have no idea what it's like to so intensely desire the simplest of things, like being able to sit across the dinner table from the person you fell in love with and hear them talk about their day or being able to curl up on the couch and enjoy the comfort of your spouse's presence while doing absolutely nothing at all. Nor do they know what it's like to constantly second-guess yourself because you no longer have that person around to make decisions with you, or to feel like you're suffocating because you no longer have someone to help you juggle the kids, household chores, and even finances, or to fight back tears during every celebratory or milestone occasion because every special moment reminds you of all that your partner is missing. They have no idea what it feels like to long for the ordinary life they shared with their spouse—because they've never had it taken away.

Losing a spouse at an early age is not something that you'd wish upon anyone, and yet you can't help but wonder if those around you might benefit from wake-up calls of their own. As you go through the motions of learning how to live without your spouse, you notice all of the things that your friends, family, and colleagues take for granted—things that *you* used to take for granted. You find yourself telling friends not to sweat the small stuff when they seem angered or annoyed by trivial things that their spouses have done and to appreciate their spouses' strengths instead of focusing on their faults. After all, if they lost their spouses tomorrow, you know they'd only remember the good times and the qualities that they fell in love with.

You also see everyone around you living as though they have all the time in the world. They put off doing, experiencing, accomplishing, and buying things with seemingly very little urgency to their lives, but you've witnessed firsthand how short life can be. Tomorrow isn't guaranteed. Your spouse didn't get the gift of time, and, even though you're suffering through moments of despair and angst and putting one foot in front of the other, trying to survive this new life of yours, there's a deeper part of you that knows life can't, or shouldn't, be taken for granted.

Yet you're existing at best—and miserable. You don't know how to change your own reality. You would like to be living more fully, but you don't know how to make your life different (or better). You have mastered the art of surviving life, silently giving yourself kudos for getting out of bed, making sure your kids are fed, paying the bills, and keeping a roof over your head. You've even learned how to do things that your spouse normally did. Still, you continue to struggle, and the sudden spells of grief keep sending you down Alice's rabbit hole, into that deep, dark, dreadful tunnel of despair. Most days, you find yourself thinking, *Will this ever get easier?*

But, as time goes on, you notice that your grief begins to change, and the intense pain in your heart starts to weaken. It doesn't fully go away, but the tsunamis of despair begin to turn into ripples. Those happy couples still remind you of what you had and make you long for the past, but you now find yourself experiencing better days in between the bad, giving you some form of emotional reprieve. As this happens, you feel sudden glimmers of hope and begin to wonder if there's a chance that you could be happy again.

Soon after the glimmers of hope begin, you grow tired of just surviving. You find yourself wanting to feel better and to move forward somehow, but you don't know how to. You don't even know what would make you happy anymore. Until recently, your world was wrapped up in someone else's. You had a title of wife or husband and someone to do things with. You had shared likes and dislikes, shared goals and dreams, and even shared hobbies. Going from two down to one was a shock, and now that you've been living in survival mode for some time, you've found yourself wondering who you even are without your other half.

You aren't the same person anymore. How could you be? But who have you become?

You start to wonder if living a life that feels better than your current reality is possible, and yet you also worry about forgetting your spouse or somehow dishonoring them in your quest to find joy without them. The thought of being happy even makes you feel a little guilty, though you know that your spouse would want you to do more than exist. They would want you to find a way to feel peace and enjoyment in life. Surely they wouldn't want their death to destroy you! And yet you still wonder, *Are my best days behind me, or can I find a way forward without forgetting?*

No, your friends and family could never fathom what it's like to walk in your shoes, handling the weight of a life meant for two, or come close to understanding the inner dialogue and questions that dance around in your mind on a daily basis. But I can.

I, too, know what it's like to live in survival mode while not wanting to take life for granted. We've both witnessed how short life can be, and while doing things without your spouse may feel pointless, I'd argue that doing nothing at all to create a better life for yourself is just as meaningless.

Yes, it wasn't supposed to be this way, and very little in your immediate world may give you reason to believe that peace and happiness are attainable now or in the foreseeable future. But know that anything is possible. Just as your world was turned upside down, it can be turned right side up. The demands of everyday life will still remain; however, I'm willing to bet that if there were a way for you to experience more ease in your life, you'd be all ears. If there were a way for you to feel better instead of experiencing all of those down days, you might listen. If there were a way for you to live a more fulfilling life while carrying your spouse with you in your heart, you'd be interested in learning how. Am I right?

If you've found yourself wondering if your best years are behind you, then I'm here to tell you that that's entirely up to you. You can choose to simply survive the rest of your days, or you can choose to honor your late spouse by living a full, meaningful, and happy life. You may not know how to do the latter just yet, but it's absolutely a choice. I know, because I made it myself.

I KNOW YOUR PAIN

I know how you feel. I know the sadness, the anger, the loneliness, and the fear in the same way that most people know their own shadows. Together, this medley of emotions took my once-confident, overachieving planner self and turned me inside out. For the first time in my life, I didn't know who I was or where I was heading. My whole world felt shattered, and I had no idea how I was supposed to pick up the pieces. I was suddenly a thirty-six-year-old single mom with no plan, and the person I used to rely on to help me figure it all out was gone.

Let me take you back to 2014, the year that would be my last with my husband. In January, when I was three months pregnant with our third child, I lost my job. My company was acquired, and my boss, the third one I'd had in my near-decade with this particular company, called to lay me off. After suffering through a script that Human Resources no doubt forced my boss to recite word for word, I hung up the phone with a heavy heart.

I had enjoyed my role as a corporate event planner and the flexibility of working remotely. It allowed me to sneak in kisses with my son, Samuel, and my daughter, Emmalyn, while I worked and to hear their giggles as my nanny played with them throughout the day. Samuel had just turned three and Emmalyn was just eighteen months, and I felt blessed to witness every first—their first roll overs, their first steps, their first words—all while getting paid to plan conferences, receptions, and forums. But as much as I loved my job, trying to find another job when I'd be going on maternity leave felt pointless.

Thankfully, my husband, Tim, agreed. He was doing well for himself as a software engineer at a defense contract company for the U.S. government and would be able to carry us financially until after the baby was born. So we decided to release our nanny, and I became a stay-at-home mom with plans to go back to event planning toward the end of that year—except that vision never came to fruition. It seems that the Universe had a different plan for us.

A few months later, in May, I had the brilliant idea

to travel back East to visit all of our friends and family —you know, since I suddenly had free time to dream up such vacations. Tim's career had brought us to Arizona, but the majority of our family and friends lived in the Northeast. Tim hesitated at first because we were down a paycheck, but my pregnancy hormones were a force to be reckoned with, and he realized that it'd be cheaper to vacation as a family of four than wait until we became a family of five. He was an engineer, remember? All of his decisions relied on logic, which often did a number on my impulsivity.

So we packed up our bags, our kids, their strollers, their diaper bags, their bottles, and their toys and headed back home, where we spent an entire week visiting almost every single person we had ever known, both on Tim's side and mine. It was heartwarming and exhausting all at once, the kind of trip that makes you want to book another vacation just to recover. But it was worth every penny. We hadn't seen our extended family and college friends in years, making the trip feel like a reunion of sorts. Little did we know that this would be the last time my husband would see any of them and the last time they'd see him alive.

In June, shortly after we got back from our whirl-wind trip, Tim started coming home from work exhausted. And by "exhausted," I mean he'd collapse on the couch soon after he walked through the door and not move until he had to go to work the following day. He had lived with Crohn's disease for years and had never experienced extreme fatigue as a symptom before, but since we couldn't think of what else it might be, he decided to reach out to his doctors to see what they thought might be going on.

I'll never forget one conversation in particular, when Tim sat across from me in our living room as I played with our kids on the floor. He had gone to the doctor's office earlier that afternoon, and when he came back, he told me that his iron levels might be low. He was going to take iron supplements with hopes that they'd lessen his fatigue, but what he said next came entirely out of left field. *"At least I'm not dying."*

The words, though uttered innocently, seemed so out of place in our living room. They even hung in the air like an echo. It was such a strange thing for Tim to say, which made me realize that he felt much worse than he was letting on.

Not long after that, Tim began consistently spiking fevers as high as 103 and 104 degrees, and the iron supplements were doing nothing to fight his fatigue. Feeling helpless, I brought Tim to the hematologist's office on a piping hot day in early July and demanded that his doctor see him immediately. It was well above 100 degrees outside, yet Tim was shivering beneath his Red Sox hoodie, seemingly getting weaker by the minute.

As we waited for the doctor, I paced the waiting room and studied my husband. He was an athletic guy. He ran half-marathons and cycled for three hours every weekend. He was strong-willed and tough, choosing to lay flagstone or build a gas firepit on his own instead of hiring someone to do it for him. But, in that doctor's office that day, he looked like a small boy, and it was unnerving to see.

All of the blood tests came up inconclusive, and my concerns were validated when the hematologist booked my husband a room at a nearby hospital. At thirty-six weeks pregnant, I wheeled my then-thirty-four-year-old husband, too weak to stand on his own, into the Tucson Medical Center with a "virus of unknown origin."

In the weeks that followed, I felt like I was living in some kind of alternate universe. I played the role of mom at home, changing diapers, giving baths, and playing with blocks while enthusiastically telling my babies that the doctors were fixing Daddy. *Soon we'll be back to normal.* Then I'd drive to the medical center, fighting back tears, and take a deep breath before plastering a hopeful smile on my face and entering Tim's hospital room.

I was trying to be strong for everyone, and it wasn't working. In fact, at one point I ended up in a hospital bed just down the hall from Tim! My blood pressure had skyrocketed under the stress of our situation and put me at risk for early labor. But as my health returned, Tim's got worse. The doctors were running hundreds of tests and still couldn't figure out what virus was taking over his body. They deemed that he needed a higher level of care, and on July 29th, just twenty-four hours before the birth of our third baby, Tim was sent two hours away to the Mayo Clinic in Scottsdale, Arizona, while I remained behind, unable to follow due to my impending labor.

As I watched the ambulance pull out of the parking lot that day, I felt sucker-punched by life. I was about to bring someone new into this world while the most critical person in my life was struggling to keep his own.

The diagnosis of Non-Hodgkin's T-Cell Lymphoma, a rare form of blood cancer that only 3% of the world gets, came days after our youngest son, Evan, was born. And while it was a blessing to finally know what was tormenting Tim's body, it was devastating just the same.

If you've ever been on a cancer journey or know someone who's been on one, then you know the ups and downs, the hope and despair, and the stress and fatigue that comes along with it.

Over the few months that followed, Tim underwent a spleen removal, multiple bone marrow biopsies, and various chemotherapy treatments, all to rid him of the cancer cells that were taking over his body. Through it all, he kept his spirits high by working remotely to stay in touch with his colleagues, watching HGTV for home improvement ideas, and walking laps around the hospital wing to keep up his strength. Even the hospital staff were impressed by him.

I, on the other hand, was falling apart. I managed to stay strong in Tim's physical presence, some days holding bags of ice in his hands as he held them outstretched over his head in physical pain and, other days, encouraging him as he shared plans to remodel our home. I purposely kept our conversations upbeat, always speaking about the future as if certain Tim would recover, never once indicating that I had any doubts. But whenever I was alone, I flip-flopped between imagining a life with Tim in it and imagining one without him. The latter was enough to bring me to my knees.

In October, Tim became a permanent resident at the Mayo Clinic, where they could closely monitor his white blood cells and give him blood transfusions as needed, and I rented a home ten minutes away with my three children and my mother-in-law. Managing an infant, a two-year-old, and a three-year-old while taking turns visiting the hospital was physically and emotionally draining, but family members would occasionally fly out to see Tim and to help us in any way they could.

It was on November 15, 2014, that my husband

received a stem cell transplant from a donor out of Europe. We nicknamed this day his "re-birth," the day his body would receive new life and the day we could finally start to recover from this exhausting journey. Our hearts were full of hope as we talked about where we'd be in one year. Ours would no doubt be a success story full of strength and determination. We were on cloud nine.

But, two weeks later, a bone marrow biopsy crushed our spirits, revealing that the cancerous cells were still present in Tim's body. And two weeks after that, I was informed via phone that they could try another chemo-therapy cocktail, which might wipe out Tim's kidneys, or they could put an end to all treatment. I was told to come to the hospital right away, as a decision needed to be made that day.

As I drove to the hospital that afternoon, panic took hold of me. I couldn't help but think, *I don't want to decide if he gets to live or die! I don't want to do this! I can't do this!* All of the months of worry and stress, of analyzing white blood cell counts, of hanging on to the doctor's every word, and of watching my husband deteriorate before my very eyes played through my mind like some horrible movie reel. I had clung to hope and prayed for a miracle, and now all I could feel was despair.

As I rode the elevator up to Tim's floor, I could feel my heart pounding in my chest. I was struggling to piece together what I might say to the man I adored, the father of my children, my best friend. I knew how much pain he was in and how much he was hurting. He wasn't the same person he had been just four months ago. He had been through hell. He was frail, bald, and beyond drained. I didn't want him to suffer anymore, and yet, selfishly, I didn't want to lose him.

As I neared Tim's room, the doctors and family members standing outside the door stepped aside to let me enter. I was surprised to find that Tim was sitting upright in his bed, waiting for me with a look of resignation on his face. I knew in that moment that he had already made up his mind. As I began to walk toward him, he looked at me with tears in his eyes and apologetically uttered the words, "I tried, babe." Instant relief and heartache swept through me simultaneously as I realized that I no longer had to decide his fate but that our life together was over. I swiftly crossed the room, wrapped my arms tightly around him, and released the tears I had been fighting back in his presence for the past five months. I knew he wanted to be free of his pain. I knew he was tired of fighting, and I couldn't blame him. But my heart was broken and I could not disguise my own pain anymore.

That night, I watched as Tim was once again escorted by ambulance—this time to a hospice center. I followed him there and realized that I needed to ask him questions no one ever thinks they'll need to ask a spouse at the age of thirty-five, like, "Where do you want to be buried?" I took the time to tell him how much I loved him, that I'd raise our kids into awesome adults, and that we'd be okay. It was the last time I'd ever see Tim conscious, and two days later, on December 14, 2014, just five months after fatigue and fevers had brought us to that hematologist's office in Tucson, he was gone.

As I knelt beside the altar at Tim's funeral, the polished titanium circle that once bound us in marriage lay on the edge of his casket. I bowed my head in disbelief for the hundredth time since his passing and let the tidal wave of sadness once again sweep through me. My heart physically ached as I picked up his ring, holding it between my fingers and thinking about all that it symbolized, and then I tucked it inside my pants pocket. That was the last time I'd ever see Tim's face, and I found myself studying it, as though trying to commit every detail of his being to memory, before closing my eyes, not wanting to face my new reality.

There are moments in life that change you, placing you on a path you never imagined yourself to be on. For us young widows and widowers, that moment was the day we lost the most important person in our world, far sooner than we ever expected to. As I said goodbye to my husband and best friend of ten years and became a young widowed mother to three small children, aged four months, two years, and three years old, my world crashed down around me and the course of my entire life—just like yours—was altered forever.

The weeks and months that followed were full of despair, uncertainty, and loneliness. I had no idea how to move forward, but I knew I needed to surround myself with some kind of support system. Given that we had no family in Arizona, I packed up our house, traveled to Rhode Island, and weeks later landed in Georgia near my father, stepmother, and sister. It was a whirlwind time for my kids and me, but Georgia became our home.

Everything seemed to pass by in a blur. I spent most of my time taking care of my children while getting settled into a new normal. In my spare time, I dutifully completed all of the tasks that surviving spouses are responsible for. I filed insurance paperwork, paid hospital bills, and sent out death certificates to my husband's various accounts, and then I began job searching.

Because I was now the sole provider for a family of four, I felt obliged to jump back into my career as a corporate event planner, despite family members telling me to take my time. I did so, hiring a daytime nanny to watch my kids. Work not only paid the bills, but it kept my mind busy during the day. At night and on the weekends, I divided my time between cooking, cleaning, and paying bills and feeding, bathing, and caring for my three kids. I was going through the motions of life but feeling completely broken inside.

When my kids were asleep at night and the house was quiet, my thoughts would immediately turn to my husband, to what we had had and what we had gone through. As I settled into an empty bed, I would think about how my life would never be the same and silently soak my pillow with tears. Some nights, my heart felt so heavy that I'd curl up on the floor of my bedroom closet where no one could hear me and sob until my head hurt. Other nights, when the tears weren't coming, I'd talk out loud to Tim and ask for his advice regarding decisions I needed to make. Almost every night, I'd ask him to give me a sign that he was still there. I needed to know that I wasn't as alone as I felt.

My friends and family, who had been super supportive in the beginning, checking in on me and making visits to Georgia when they could, all went back to their own lives, and I couldn't blame them. This was my journey to sort out, not theirs. But I was on my own for the first time in a decade, this time with three small children in tow. All I could manage to do was put one foot in front of the other.

As you know, when you go from having your future mapped out with someone else to having your world upended in the middle of your life, you also start to question everything. I began to question whether I was making the right choices for myself and my kids, whether we'd be okay, and whether I'd ever be happy again. Being a solo parent, working full-time, and managing a house all on my own felt overwhelming and harder than anything I had ever done before.

During this time, I'd drop Samuel off at preschool and then sit in my car and watch as other children's dads brought their children in and out of the daycare building. I'd feel a tidal wave of sadness wash over me. Everything had become something Tim wouldn't get to do, something he was missing out on, or something my kids wouldn't get to experience. Even during school functions, as other happy parents gleefully videotaped their sons and daughters singing silly holiday songs with their classes, I stood there fighting to keep the floodgates from opening while managing a small smile for Samuel. It all seemed so unfair. I found myself growing resentful of happy families simply because they had the life I had once had, the life I would have given anything to have back.

Being widowed changes you in more ways than you'd think, though, doesn't it? Confidence falls to the wayside, self-doubt creeps into its place, and even the most extroverted among us start to feel a bit intro-verted. I felt like an outsider everywhere I went. None of my friends were widowed, and coworkers all had spouses to go home to (or so it seemed). Even those who were divorced still had another person on this planet available to help them make decisions regarding their children. I felt like no one could possibly understand what I was going through or relate to my life in the slightest way, so I kept to myself.

I found myself alternating between bouts of despair and anger most days. I knew I needed to heal, but I didn't know how. So I started going to grief counseling on my lunch break. Three different grief counselors, to be exact. One told me that it was good to have feelings, and another handed me a piece of paper with the five stages of grief listed on it. I stopped going. I knew I was sad. I knew I was angry and resentful. I wanted someone to pull me out of the negative emotions I was living in, not acknowledge them.

My kids were still under the age of five at this point, and while I continued to survive each day, I began to wonder if I was doing enough to help them process their own grief. My youngest mostly ate, played, and threw tantrums, as toddlers do, but my daughter, Emmalyn, and my oldest son, Samuel, teetered between okay and not okay. Samuel, for one, repeatedly asked me when Daddy was coming home. His deeper concern was revealed to me one night as I was putting him to bed. Noticing a small cut on my thumb about the size of a paper cut, he reminded me that "Daddy's blood was sick." He then got really quiet and asked, "What if something happens to you? You're the only parent we have left."

My heart broke into a million pieces as the words

fell out of Samuel's tiny mouth. He was only four years old, and the worry seemed too big for his body. I reassured him that I was not sick and that I would be around for a long time, but as we continued to talk about his dad and what had happened to him, he suddenly grew quieter and added, "I never got to say goodbye."

The pain of his statement sent ripples through my heart because it was true. My kids were not allowed on the cancer floor of the Mayo Clinic, and I had not brought them to hospice. I hadn't wanted them to see their father lying there unconscious. It dawned on me at that moment that they had never gotten the closure that I had gotten. So I told Samuel that his dad could still hear him and that we could say goodbye together, right then and there. I laid down next to Samuel in his twin-sized bed, and, as tears streamed down my cheeks, we stared at the ceiling and said, "Goodbye, Daddy" in unison.

Not long after that, when Samuel entered kindergarten, his teacher asked to meet with me. Together with the school counselor, she informed me that Samuel's behavior was a bit concerning. He was crawling around on the schoolroom floor, sitting across the room from his peers during "circle time," and chewing on everything from his shirt collar to pencils. I began to cry as I told them about his dad, and they handed me a box of tissues as they suggested I enroll Samuel in play therapy.

I had no idea what play therapy was, but I now know that it involves a lot of imaginative play and role-play, which helps kids talk about their feelings in a way that feels safe to them. The therapists will use all kinds of activities to do this, including art, games, and music, but the one tool I found to be most intriguing, and the one that Samuel gravitated toward, was the sand table. Apparently all play therapists have one! It looks just like a sandbox that you might see at a playground, except it's on table legs and in an office. Your child essentially gets to play with toys and figurines in the sand while the therapist gets them to act out what's going on in their subconscious mind. This is how Samuel ultimately shared his thoughts on the loss of his dad.

I remember getting a phone call from Samuel's play therapist while I was executing an international conference in San Diego one particular September afternoon. Samuel had graduated to first grade by then and had been in therapy for an entire year. In school, he was learning how all stories have a beginning, a middle, and an end, and so he told the therapist that he was going to share a story with her. He began creating a scene in the sand with "good guys" and "bad guys" and got halfway through an intense plot between good and evil when the therapist, eyeing the clock, told him they'd need to finish up soon in order to end their session on time. But Samuel insisted that all stories must have endings and continued on despite her warning. He placed all the good guys and bad guys back in their original spots and said, "See? All they ever really wanted was for things to go back to the way they were in the beginning."

As the therapist relayed Samuel's story to me, amazed at how well he articulated his feelings using a metaphor, I burst into tears in the middle of the Hilton San Diego Bayfront hotel lobby. My heart longed for the past, too, and I was crushed that I couldn't put everything back into place for him. *For us.*

My daughter Emmalyn had started transitional kindergarten that year, and her pent-up emotions about the loss of her dad also began to bubble to the surface. Except, instead of withdrawing and chewing on everything, as Samuel had done, Emmalyn was full of rage. She threw chairs across her classroom, crawled under tables, and went on rampages through the school, tearing things off the walls as she went. I was getting calls from the principal almost every other day, and I didn't know what to do. So I enrolled Emmalyn in play therapy too, and prayed for answers.

My world was falling apart at the seams. I was doing my best to stay afloat, both at work and at home, but Samuel and Emmalyn were struggling, and I felt like I was drowning. I wanted to believe that there were better days ahead and that we weren't destined for a life of hardship and misery. I wanted to know that we'd manage to find a healthy way forward and that we'd all eventually make peace with our situation and learn to be happy despite our devastating loss. But all I could manage to do was get through each day as I grappled with despair, anger, loneliness, and fear and prayed we'd eventually have a life worth living again.

HOW DOES ONE RECOVER FROM THIS?

At some point, you get tired of just surviving your loss. You get tired of grieving, and you want to find joy in life again, even if you don't know how to.

This happens to almost every widow and widower I've ever spoken with. I reached this point after a whirlwind year of struggling to keep myself and my kids in one piece. For me, it was right before the first anniversary of Tim's death, but the timing is different for everyone. Widows and widowers have joined my private Facebook group, Widows & Widowers Seeking Happiness, to move forward, feel better, and have lives worth living again as little as six weeks and as many as ten years out from their loss.

We all seem to experience a turning point or a "shift," a moment when we decide that enough is enough. While we still love and miss our spouse, we begin to think, *I'm tired of feeling this way*, or, *I'm tired of living this way*. My moment came while I was on a business trip.

As an event manager, I would often fly to various cities throughout the United States to execute conferences, trade shows, and various meetings. On one particular trip, I found myself drawn to a newsstand full of books outside a convenience shop in the Hartsfield-Jackson Atlanta International Airport. It wasn't unusual for me to pick up a froofy fiction novel to escape into on a flight. But that day, I picked up a book that would wind up creating an internal shift within me and inspiring my climb out of survival mode. It was a nonfiction story about a neurosurgeon who had experienced "the afterlife" during a near-death experience.

Mind you, I was still grieving the life I had had and missing Tim terribly. But as I read the back cover of this book, which talked about the neurosurgeon's journey beyond this world during a seven-day coma, it gave me hope that there was something bigger than us at play. And this was a time when I desperately needed to believe that.

I devoured the doctor's story on that flight, and as I started to imagine reuniting with Tim in a world beyond our own, my inner world began to change. I was reminded of my promise to him during our final hours together in hospice and how I had vowed to raise our kids to become awesome adults. I had also promised Tim that our kids and I would be okay. As I closed the book, I decided that it was time for me to make good on that promise.

To be clear, this particular book did not give me any tools or advice on how to move forward after loss. Rather, it made me question how our universe operates, why we're all here, and what my own purpose for still being here was as a young widowed mom. These questions planted seeds of curiosity within me, setting me on a new path, and ultimately launched my desire to climb out of survival mode.

For the first time, I viewed Tim's death as a wake-up call. Up until then, I had been moseying through life. Even in our marriage, we always spoke about our dream home, things we wished to see, or vacations we wanted to take in terms of "someday" or "one day." I'm willing to bet that you and your spouse did the same! But Tim never got to see or do any of our "someday" plans. His life had been ripped away from him at the early age of thirty-five.

As I closed the book, still asking those big questions, I was reminded that tomorrow is not guaranteed. Tim's cancer journey was proof. Tim's cancer had taken his life in less than six months. Knowing this, I felt I had a choice to make. I could choose to continue shuffling through my days, feeling sad and angry over what I had lost, or I could choose to make some positive changes and live an extraordinary life in honor of Tim.

I desperately wanted the latter, and I knew Tim would have wanted me to make that choice, too. The problem was, I didn't know where or how to begin. My days were still split between working, managing an entire house, and taking care of three kids under the age of five. On top of that, I was flip-flopping between sadness and anger, and I had no idea how to create balance in my life, never mind find joy in it. Can you relate?

But the spark had been lit, and so I became determined to find a way forward. What transpired over the next few years happened because of that single decision, and it's one that I feel we all have to make. At some point, we all must decide whether we're going to remain victims of our circumstances or participants in our own rescue.

I had unconsciously played the victim for over a year. I had allowed myself to wallow in self-pity, to feel alone instead of connecting with others, to let self-doubt replace confidence, and to stay stuck in negative patterns. But, as you'll learn in the next chapters, we are all capable of creating full and happy lives despite how devastating our losses were, and if you make the choice to move forward, peace and joy are absolutely attainable. *Yes, even for you!*

The next several years were a monumental self-help

journey for me. Determined to pick up the pieces of my life and to make something extraordinary out of it, I began reading when my kids were asleep, listening to audiotapes on my lunch breaks, and attending seminars whenever possible. I turned to metaphysics, mindfulness, and all kinds of strategies and techniques from spiritual gurus like Wayne Dyer, Deepak Chopra, Rhonda Byrne, Esther Hicks, and Eckhart Tolle, looking for answers, ways to elevate my spirit, and anything that might help me. I even used tools from leaders like Tony Robbins and Dean Graziosi to gain clarity during a time when I had no idea what would even make me happy anymore. I tried everything these knowledgeable teachers suggested, and then I tossed what didn't work for me and kept what did.

It took me four to five years to climb out of survival mode, and in the coming chapters I will share the strategies, techniques, and tools I used to do it. It wasn't always easy. Triggers and challenges often led me astray, causing me to "forget" what I was learning and to regress some, but then I'd remember my promise to Tim and get myself back on track. Do I still miss my husband? Of course I do. But I am also happy and thriving on my own. And you can be, too.

There was a point in my widowhood journey when I did not think my little family would come out the other side of grief. The struggles and the trials seemed too large, and they seemed to last for an eternity. In those early years, I felt like we were on a sinking ship, but I was determined to steer us forward. I became adamant about keeping my promise to my husband, and so I strengthened my bond with each of my children and got them the help that they needed while I implemented new practices and techniques to close the gap from where I was to where I wanted to be. I would have given anything to fast-forward and know that we were going to be okay throughout the process, so today, as you read this, I'm telling you: *You are going to be okay*.

I know your loss is devastating. Mine was, too. But in time, the intense pain you're feeling will lessen. Achieving happiness, on the other hand, will require a bit of intentionality. You can't continue to do the same things you're doing now over and over again and expect to one day wake up happy.

With that said, you have a decision to make—the same one I had to make. You can continue to remain a victim of your circumstances, like I did for so long, or you can choose to become the hero of your own life story. Which would your spouse want for you?

The good news is that, if you've hit your turning point—if you want to climb out of survival mode and accelerate your journey toward peace and happiness— you're about to learn a slew of strategies that will help you do just that. But you must choose to participate in your own rescue. I can give you the techniques and tools to help you find your way, but you are the one who must do the work.

I've done the work in my own life, and if I can do it with three little ones in tow, I have no doubt you can do it, too. You are absolutely capable of creating a life worth living again—and you can do it while carrying your spouse with you in your heart. Are you ready?

FROM SURVIVING TO THRIVING

Throughout the rest of this book, I'm going to teach you the key techniques, tools, and practices that helped me get to the great place I'm in today. I'm actually going to teach them to you in the way that I wish I had learned them. If you recall, my journey took four to five years. That's because my quest for answers took me all over the place, and I tried many things that didn't work. This book is a compilation of the strategies that *did* work, and it's my goal to help you to get closer to peace and joy more quickly than I did.

However, this is going to involve some work on your part. What you're about to learn will require practice, rumination, and even a bit of contemplation. In fact, you should probably grab a notebook and a pen so that you can take notes and do the exercises as you read them. I promise they will do wonders for your progress forward. You want to participate in your own rescue, right? Then go grab that pen and paper!

Before I go any further, let me explain the journey you're about to embark upon. There are quite a few things that widows and widowers can do to start creating better realities for themselves, and the first, which I'll cover in Chapter 5, has to do with focus.

It is really hard to move in a forward direction when you're looking backward. Sounds obvious, right? You wouldn't drive a car while staring in the rearview mirror or ride a bike while looking over your back shoulder, would you?

When you're grief-stricken over the loss of a spouse, it can be hard to think about the future, especially when nothing looks or feels the same anymore. Trust me, I know. Objects around the house, songs on the radio, and even comments made by innocent strangers are enough to keep your thoughts locked on the past. But this won't move you forward. You cannot create a better reality for yourself if you're solely focused on what you no longer have in your life. You must learn to carry the memories of your spouse with you as you readjust your focus to the present, and I'm going to help you do that.

In Chapter 6, you'll learn to feel relief from your grief in a matter of minutes. This is something that I wish I had learned early on as a widow! Of course, we all must go through the grieving process and it's okay —and normal!—to feel sad, depressed, and even angry on your journey. But when you've hit your turning point, the moment when you think enough is enough, trying to switch gears and elevate your emotions can feel a bit arduous.

What if I told you that, when you're feeling sad, angry, or resentful (like I was), it's often because of the stories you're telling yourself? Think about it: If you're thinking, *I can't do this on my own*, how are you feeling at that moment? Chances are good that your emotions are mirroring that thought. And, when you're feeling low, how likely are you to take positive action? Not likely. That's because the stories we tell ourselves impact both the way we feel and the actions we take. If you can change the story going on in your mind, you can change your emotional state and start taking more positive actions. How do you change your story? I'm going to teach you how in Chapter 6!

Once you're forward-focused and feeling some emotional relief, we're going to hone in on your "why." That will be in Chapter 7. Your "why" is the reason you want to climb out of survival mode. Maybe you want to set a great example for your kids or honor your spouse by living more fully. Or maybe you don't yet know your "why," but you know you can't continue to live this way. That's okay. I'm going to help you figure it out because it's important to understand your "why" before you try to make changes in your life. Once you've got it, it will empower you, inspire you, and motivate you to action.

You might be thinking, *What action? I don't even know what I want!* Don't worry, I didn't either. When I began my soul-searching journey, I had no idea what might bring me joy going forward. All of my plans had involved my husband in some way, and now that I was on my own, I was merely trying to survive. Family, friends, and colleagues had five-year goals. I was living day-to-day.

But, as world-renowned author and coach Tony Robbins says, *clarity is power.* In Chapter 8, I'm going to walk you through several different exercises—ones that I've used myself—to help you get clear on where you're going. I'm going to get you thinking beyond today and even next week!

Think of each exercise as a brainstorm of sorts. They are designed to help you identify the kinds of things you wish to do, see, or have and to help you pinpoint what you want for yourself, your kids, your work, your health, and your overall lifestyle. This might feel difficult at first. I've had clients tell me that thinking beyond the present was just too hard. But I encourage you to stick with me and to complete the exercises to the best of your ability. This process helped me rediscover desires I had long forgotten about, and you might be surprised at what comes up for you, too.

Plus, you'll need to complete the exercises in order to move on to Chapter 9, which is where we'll create an action plan.

That's right! In Chapter 9, we're going to take the list of desires you came up with and chunk them down into small, actionable steps! Why? Because making progress toward newly identified goals is what's going to help you climb out of survival mode and move toward thriving. Uncovering what might make you happy is the first step. The second is taking positive action that will help you create a life that feels good again. Don't worry, I have a tool that will help you do this, and I'll be holding your hand throughout the whole process.

In Chapter 10, I'm going to share a plethora of practices that will help create a positive shift in your life and then keep the massive positive momentum going. These are not related to the stories you tell yourself or the new goals you will be going after. Instead, they relate to your holistic well-being and can be used daily to bring you closer to inner peace and happiness. I have used all of the practices I'm about to share and they have all worked for me. I'm going to ask you to try each of them to see what works for you.

You may be thinking, *I have no time for new goals or new "practices,"* to which my response is: You can *always* make time for the things that are important to you.

The question becomes, *How important is finding joy in life again?*

So often, humans (not just widows and widowers) spend time on things that don't serve them or move them forward in any way. Huge chunks of time are lost, and this can keep you stuck or feeling "in a rut." But there are ways to create little bits of time for the things that will move you forward, and, in Chapter 11, I'm going to share some of those ways with you.

By Chapter 12, you will know how to feel relief from those tidal waves of grief, you'll have remembered what makes you *you*, you'll have an idea of what's going to make you happy on your own, you'll have created an action plan to get there, you'll have some healthy new habits that are making you feel better every day, and you'll be building positive momentum in your life. How does that sound?

Of course, there will still be bumps on your journey, just like there were on mine, and so Chapter 12 is all about giving yourself grace. There will always be good days and bad, but I promise that the good days will start to outnumber the bad. Try not to lose sight of the overall progress you're making, and keep using the techniques and practices you learn here to continue moving yourself forward.

It goes without saying that you didn't ask to become widowed, but you are fully capable of finding joy in life again despite your loss. You may have picked up this book desiring hope and a bit of inspiration, but you deserve more than that. You deserve a fulfilling and happy life. It is my wish to guide you on a positive path forward and to show you just how strong and resilient you can be. I've titled Chapter 13 "This Is Your Comeback Story" because you're about to embark on one, and I'm incredibly honored to be part of your journey.

This may all sound like a major undertaking, and skepticism, hesitancy, or doubt may be sweeping through your mind, causing you to question whether the strategies in this book will work for you. You may even be thinking, *This will be good to know someday, later, when I'm ready for it!* Recognize that this is just fear talking and ask yourself, *If not now, then when?* Besides, how will you know until you try? Will there ever be a perfect moment?

Remember, I was far from okay once, too. I've been you. And I want nothing more than to see your heart smile again—sooner rather than later. How we became widowed may not be the same and our living situations may look entirely different, but I started my journey in the same dark place as you. I don't have to know the details of your path to know your struggles. I know your pain, intimately, and if I could make everything right in your world by simply wrapping my arms around you in a bear hug, I would. *In a heartbeat.*

But life is moving forward. It's not waiting for you to be ready. You've got a lot of days left to live, and as much as I'd love to pull you forward to a better place by doing the work for you, this is something you must do yourself, *for* yourself. I can only show you how to get from where you are to where you'd like to be. What you do with this information is entirely up to you.

I know where you are, and I also know what's on the other side of that dark place. There's peace and love and a different kind of happy. *You can get there.* We *all* have the ability to triumph over tragedy. It doesn't matter who you are or what you've been through. Even if you don't feel strong at this very moment, I promise you that your strength is there, waiting for you to call upon it. I assure you that I did not feel strong as a newly widowed mom, trying to balance a career with a baby, a toddler, and a preschooler while grieving the loss of my husband. Yet I, along with many of the widows and widowers who I have worked with, have found the inner strength to move forward using many of the tools and practices you're about to learn. You can too, if you choose to.

It's all a choice. You can choose to linger in despair for a few more weeks, months, or years, or you can decide right now that you want to grow from your loss and find your way forward. You can choose to become bitter, or you can decide to move in the direction of peace. You can choose to do very little at all, or you can decide to take baby steps forward toward a life that will feel ten times better and make your spouse super proud. You and only you can make these choices, and the decision you make right now could be life changing.

As Tony Robbins likes to say, "Ten years from now you will surely arrive. The question is: Where?"

Everything you read beyond this page will help you mend your heart, rediscover yourself, evolve, and rebuild your life, *if you choose to do the work*. That means committing to this process and doing each exercise, as honestly and authentically as you can. It means giving each practice your all, however imperfectly. It does not mean skimming through the tools and practices half-heartedly or with a plan to do them later, maybe, if you get around to them. Your life will not get better by chance! It will only get better when you make little changes here and there that will create the positive shift you're craving.

So what do you say? Are you ready to make today Day One of your journey out of survival mode? Are you ready to commit to making yourself a priority and making the rest of your life count? If so, try to let go of all the negative self-talk that's been filling you up with self-doubt and put down your excuses, including the infamous "no time" one. Ask yourself, *Do I want to be in this same place next year?* Plan to wake up fifteen minutes earlier a few mornings a week, record your favorite TV shows instead of watching them live, or hire a sitter for a few hours. Do whatever it takes to make this investment in yourself because *you are worth it.*

It's time to get unstuck. It's time to climb out of survival mode once and for all. It's time to learn how to enjoy life again, on your own. You can do this, and I am going help you. Are you ready to begin your transformation? Good. Then let's get started.

5

WHERE'S YOUR FOCUS?

One of the hardest parts about moving forward and rebuilding your life after loss is learning how to focus on the here and now without constantly ruminating over the past and how life was supposed to be. This is incredibly difficult to do! I spent over a year trying to process what had just happened and feeling resentful toward life for taking my husband away, turning my world upside down, and seemingly giving me more than I could handle. But when I decided to make good on my promise to Tim that the kids and I would be okay, I knew I had to let that all go.

You can't possibly forge ahead and rebuild a happy life for yourself when you're solely focused on what was, what isn't, or what should have been. Remember how we talked about not driving a car while staring in the rearview mirror? You must learn to glance at the rearview mirror, or process, reflect on, and appreciate what you once had while fixing your eyes on the road ahead. It's the only way you'll be able to create a life that feels good to you again.

I know that life didn't turn out the way that you wanted it to. I've walked the same path as you. But your life is far from over and if you want to find joy in life again, then you must begin to loosen your grip on the past and accept the present in whatever way you can. If you find yourself struggling to do this, or if you're somewhere between longing for the good ol' days and wanting to find a way forward, then, at best, you'll *survive* life—you won't thrive. Embracing the present, even with its current imperfections, is the only way to begin moving out of survival mode and toward a life worth living.

To be clear, moving forward does not mean moving on. So many of the widows and widowers in my Facebook group, Widows & Widowers Seeking Happiness, fear that, if they turn their attention all the way forward, their memories will fade, or worse, disappear. I assure you that this will not happen. At the time of this writing, it has been six-and-a-half years since Tim's passing and I can still recall every detail of his being and relive images captured in photos like they happened yesterday. I can even recall the sound of his voice and the way he fondly called me "babe." None of that goes away. You simply learn to carry your spouse and the life you shared with you as you march forward and live in a way that would make them proud.

Remember, your spouse wouldn't have wanted their death to destroy you, and while I know you are hurting, please hear this: This is not the end of your story! You still have a lot of life left to live. How your life unfolds from this point forward will depend largely on where you place your focus. If you choose to remain fixated on the past, staring in that rearview mirror, then chances are high that you will stay stuck, even if, on some level, you wish to be happy again. If, however, you choose to carry the memories of your spouse with you and turn your attention to what you still have and where you're headed, as I did, then you will begin to move away from despair and toward happiness. Even if you're not sure what you want for yourself just yet, accepting your reality and choosing to direct your attention ahead—through the front windshield!—is an important first step. Later, we'll get clear on what might make you happy!

Why is your focus so important? Because energy flows where attention goes. Have you ever noticed that you're constantly getting what you're thinking about? I once spent an entire day proving this. I decided to take something I didn't care about—tan cars—and I focused all of my attention on spotting them for eight straight hours. Everywhere I went that day—on highways, down side streets, in parking garages, and in parking lots—I zoned right in on tan cars. And wouldn't you know, I saw hundreds of them! Had I not been looking for them, I wouldn't have noticed them at all. Normally my brain wouldn't have pointed the tan cars out to me, but because I directed my focus on them, they appeared everywhere!

The same applies to the journey you're on and your healing process. Not only do you bring what you focus on into your awareness, but you *feel* what you focus on. Have you ever noticed that, when you're focused on the past and reliving the way things used to be in your mind, a song your spouse used to love plays on the radio, everyone seems to be talking about their partners, and even household chores bring back memories of shared responsibilities? This makes you feel very alone and sad. On the other hand, when you turn your focus to the present or toward the future, you become aware of opportunities you didn't see before, you go out more with friends and family, and you begin to work on your health or complete house projects that you weren't motivated to do before. You feel more hopeful and even optimistic.

Where you choose to focus will influence how you

use your energy—in a positive or negative way—and that impacts the results you get in life. Dean Graziosi illustrates this perfectly through the following story, which he shares in a program he teaches with Tony Robbins called the Knowledge Broker Blueprint.

As part of a church program one summer, a group of dads from a community church took their twenty teenage boys on a whitewater rafting adventure trip to Colorado. Prior to their arrival in the Centennial State, it had rained for four straight days, causing river conditions to become extremely dangerous. On the day of their excursion, the rapids were approaching a Class V status, and everyone was suddenly nervous.

The dads considered canceling the rafting adventure, but then their guide came out and put them all at ease as he said, "Dads, relax. Boys, get in the raft! We're going to be just fine."

The guide held up his pointer finger and said, "You see this finger? It's the Positive Point. I want you to focus all of your energy wherever I point. Paddle your guts out in that direction, and I promise we'll be safe. I've never lost anyone!"

He went on to explain to the dads that, when he first became a guide, he'd notice a really bad rapid and yell, "Boys, don't go to that rapid or we'll flip over!" Or he'd see a fallen-down tree or a rock in the middle of the river and exclaim, "Don't hit that tree! Don't hit that rock!" Sure enough, everyone would turn, look at the rapid, tree, or rock, run right into it, and flip over.

"I realized that what we focus on is where we go," the guide said. Now, he points his finger where he wants the group to go, and they put all of their energy and focus there. In turn, they make it to their destination, bypassing all of the obstacles without ever knowing they were even there!

I tell you Dean's story because, so often, when we're focusing on the past and what we no longer have and feeling sad or depressed about it, we're directing all of our energy toward the things we don't want in life— so we end up getting more of what we don't want! Case in point: if you're constantly focused on how you no longer have your spouse's help as you juggle a career and a family on your own, you're likely to feel a lot of despair and overwhelm. And, if you're in a constant state of despair and overwhelm, are you more likely to go down Alice's rabbit hole, that pit of sorrow that's so hard to climb out of, or to create some time for self-care? Chances are you'll go down Alice's rabbit hole, neglecting some of your duties at work or at home in the process and causing them to pile up—thus creating even less time for yourself, which is what you don't want!

You can't attract or begin to create a better-feeling life if you're focused on what you don't want. It's like staring directly at the bad rapid, the fallen-down tree, or the rock in the middle of the river and placing all of your energy on it, all the while hoping that you'll skirt right past it or miraculously find yourself on a calmer river in a different state. It doesn't work that way! You of course run right into each obstacle, falling down Alice's rabbit hole as you go, and then continue to direct your attention toward what you don't want in every other area of your life: your home life, your health, your work, and even your relationships. You don't even realize you're doing it! You just find yourself thinking, *My life sucks!*

But it doesn't have to be that way. When you can change your focus and place your attention on what you still have and what you want for yourself, you'll be able to see past the bad rapids, the fallen-down trees, and the rocks that have threatened to keep you stuck until this very moment. You'll start to see opportunities instead of obstacles because you'll be channeling your overall energy toward creating a better-feeling life. You'll even wake up earlier or stay up later to practice self-care, thus creating some much-needed time for yourself!

Even if you don't completely know what you want, you can begin to make a positive shift by turning your attention to what you still have instead of focusing on what you don't. One way I like to do this is by practicing gratitude, the act of being thankful for the blessings in your life. When you spend just a few minutes each day being grateful for what you already have, you will begin to reap all kinds of benefits.

"What constitutes a blessing when you're grieving?" you ask.

Anything and everything that brings color to your life right now or makes you feel safe or at peace in some way is a blessing. Uncovering these may feel challenging at first. After all, learning to recognize all that you're blessed with when your heart is longing for what is gone is not easy. I know. I've been there. Some widows and widowers even feel guilty for appreciating the good in their lives.

I've had one client tell me he felt like he was dishonoring his spouse by appreciating what was good in his world. Please do not feel guilty! Guilt is an emotion that we place upon ourselves because we think we should or should not be doing something. I assure you that your spouse would want you to heal, to grow, and to continue living. Appreciating the people, places, and things that make life bearable or even enjoyable in this moment is part of that process. So if you are struggling with guilt, try to remember that honoring your spouse and appreciating your life is not an either/or situation. In fact, your spouse would want you to find a way to honor them while appreciating the life that you get to live.

If finding blessings to be grateful for still feels difficult to you, then try thinking about what you have in your life right now that would be hard to live without. Maybe it's the roof over your head, your career, your paycheck, your kids, or the friend who always listens when something triggers your grief. I had one widow tell me that, when she started this practice, she literally wrote down the words "toothbrush," "toothpaste," and "pencil." She was feeling so low that she couldn't appreciate much else. Over time, she of course found more and more to be grateful for and even told me that she found the practice to be quite healing.

Appreciating what's right in your world, no matter how minuscule each gratitude may seem to you, will help train your brain to see even more positives in your life. It's like the exercise I did with the tan cars. I had never paid attention to tan cars before in my life, but once I focused my attention on them, I saw them everywhere that I looked.

Training your brain to seek out blessings will make you feel good, too. The act of being thankful releases dopamine and serotonin in your brain. Dopamine is the same endorphin that gives runners that infamous "runner's high" and serotonin helps activate the happy center of your brain! Who doesn't want to activate the happy center of their brain? And, as if that's not reason enough to practice gratitude, the act of being thankful will also help you replace negative emotions with more positive ones, express more compassion toward yourself and others, increase your self-esteem, decrease your stress, and even improve your sleep!

Practicing gratitude doesn't even have to take long. There are so many ways to incorporate thankfulness into your everyday life. You could keep a gratitude journal and write in it every night before bed, or keep a running list that you add to throughout your day, or simply notice things that you're grateful for without writing anything down at all. There is no right or wrong way to practice gratitude, but it's important to note that you must feel emotion when you're doing it. If you don't feel positive emotions of any kind during your gratitude practice, you'll reap none of the benefits I mentioned above. Remember, you want to learn to appreciate the positives in your life so that you can begin to refocus your energy on moving forward and experiencing happiness again. Writing a list for the sake of checking a box on your to-do list won't activate the happy center of your brain!

I know people who keep a gratitude journal by their bedside and people who practice gratitude in their heads. My gratitude practice has varied a lot over the years. When I first started practicing, I wrote down a list of the people, places, things, and situations I encountered that I felt deeply grateful for each day, with zero regard to meeting any kind of set number. That meant that some days I listed ten things and other days I struggled to come up with three. As my kids grew and life got busier, and when writing my list became a chore, I switched to practicing gratitude while I exercised. I'd often be walking on my treadmill or running at a nearby trail for thirty to sixty minutes multiple times a week, so I chose to spend a portion of that time focusing my attention on what was going right for me. I have since changed my practice once again, spending just two minutes a day (sometimes multiple times a day!) closing my eyes and leaning into my heart as I think about the people and things that light up my world. As a result, I'm more aware of positive moments and positive experiences in my life versus the negative ones I focused on as a newer widow.

Again, practicing gratitude can be done in whatever way works best for you, but I encourage you to try it once a day for at least two weeks. It only takes a few minutes and it will help you redirect your focus from the past to the present. Your list doesn't even have to be long; it just needs to mean something to you.

Over time, as you continue this practice, you'll notice that you're able to appreciate more and more aspects of your life. That's because, as you turn your focus from what's missing to what's going right, you begin to notice all of the things you couldn't see before. It's hard to see the blessings when we're focused on the past and even harder to move forward toward happiness when we're focused on what isn't happy in our lives. But if you can learn to catch yourself staring in that rearview mirror and use gratitude to bring you back to the present, and if you can carry the memories of your spouse with you while appreciating everything you still have today, you will begin attracting even more opportunities for gratitude into your world while beginning the process of creating a better future.

6

CHANGE YOUR STORY, CHANGE YOUR LIFE

One of the most important lessons I have learned as a widow is to watch my thoughts (or at least be aware of them). Why? Because everything we feel is related to our thoughts.

In my signature course, *How to Enjoy Life + Be Happy Again: Strategies for Young Widows + Widowers,* I ask my students to spend an entire week monitoring their emotions. Every time they feel sad, deflated, lonely, or full of self-doubt, I ask that they simply notice their thoughts in those moments and write them down. I then ask each of them to tell me what emotions they felt most consistently throughout the week, or most often, and what thoughts they noticed each time. Most of the time, they report feeling "sadness" or "despair," and typical thought patterns include "I can't do this without my spouse" or "My life sucks." I'm willing to bet you have these thoughts, too.

I then ask, "What did you do when you felt this way?"

As you can imagine, most go down Alice's rabbit hole and lose all motivation to do anything at all. That's because we act out the stories we tell ourselves.

Your emotions are a direct result of your thoughts. Think about it: you can't tell yourself that life is hard and feel happy. Even further, your emotions dictate how you behave. So if you're thinking that your life is hard and feeling bad about it, you're not going to do the same things you'd do if you were thinking that your life is easy and feeling good! When you're thinking negative thoughts and feeling hopeless, you tend to lose all motivation to complete basic household tasks or even go to work. One client of mine, whom I'll call Adam, was missing work for days on end because he was in such a state of despair. But when you're thinking better thoughts and feeling optimistic, you will do the opposite. You might plow through your list of weekend chores, finish that house project your spouse once started, or even apply for a better job.

Not only do your emotions dictate what you do and don't do, but your behavior impacts the results you get in life. For instance, if you're feeling sad and doing nothing to better your situation, you will continue to experience your life as it is today, day after day.

However, if you're feeling slightly hopeful and start taking baby steps forward, then you will begin to experience a different reality. After Adam began monitoring his thoughts in an effort to feel better, he was able to take more inspired action. In fact, he stopped skipping work and even landed a more fulfilling job less than six months later!

Do you see the domino effect? Your thoughts influence your emotions, which dictate your behavior, and your behavior impacts the results you get in life.

It all starts with your thoughts, and, so often, our thoughts are just stories we somehow picked up on our life paths. They can be stories we've been telling ourselves since childhood, like "I'm a failure," or ones that we've just recently started telling ourselves out of fear, like "I can't do this on my own."

The problem is that when you're telling yourself that "life sucks," life is going to continue to feel like it sucks! Believing a story like that is like trying to drive a car with a flat tire. You'll go nowhere.

So how can you change the stories you tell yourself?

Becoming aware of them is a start. To do this, I encourage you to try the exercise I give my students. Spend a week noting your thoughts whenever you're feeling low and try to identify what triggered the emotions. What were you thinking? What story were you telling yourself?

Also notice how the thoughts impacted your behavior. What did you do next? Did you throw yourself a pity party? Did you indulge in some not-so-healthy comfort food? Did you take it out on your kids? Did you lose all motivation for the day?

When you become aware of your thoughts, you'll start to notice specific stories that keep coming up for you. This is important because you can begin to shift them to something more positive once you're aware of them. And, when you turn them into something more positive, you'll not only feel better, but you'll begin taking more positive action. Basically, when you change your stories, you start to change your life!

One of my clients, whom I'll call Paige, was living with a myriad of negative stories and wondering why she was having trouble moving forward as a young widow. She came to me less than a year out from the loss of her husband and told me that she wanted to build up her confidence and learn to be okay on her own.

Paige was living with her parents and her two young boys at the time, and she was getting ready to move out on her own. She confessed that she had never lived without her parents or her husband and was worried that she wouldn't be able to handle being on her own. She wanted to feel more confident, happy, and secure, but in reality, she felt scared, anxious, and lonely.

When I asked Paige what she thought when she felt those scared, anxious, and lonely feelings, here's what she had to say: "My life sucks and always will. I'll always be treading water. My life will never be whole or complete again. I'll never be comfortable alone."

Can you see how these stories, or limiting beliefs, could keep someone stuck instead of empowering them to rebuild an extraordinary life?

I walked Paige through each of her disempowering thought patterns and simply asked her if they were true. For example, did she really think her life would *always* suck? I asked her to recall previous times when life hadn't gone her way and helped her to realize that she had always managed to get to a better place. I then challenged her thoughts on being uncomfortable alone by asking if she would still feel uneasy with a great job, perfect health, hobbies and friendships that fulfilled her, a home that she loved, and a life full of new adventures with her boys. Without hesitation, she answered, "No."

As I questioned her stories, they began to lose power. And as they lost power, Paige realized that she could choose to believe something different. She could choose to tell herself a different story, a more empowering one. And with more empowering beliefs, she could more easily boost her confidence, reduce her anxiety, and do more for herself to feel less lonely. Today, Paige owns a home that she loves, is physically active and engaged in hobbies, is going for her master's degree, and is setting an amazing example for her boys!

This is my hope for you.

As you start to move forward, pay attention to the stories you tell yourself and remember: they're just stories. Ask yourself if they're true and then try to shift them to something more positive. In doing so, you'll start to feel some emotional relief, which will allow you to begin taking more positive action in your life.

It's important to note that this isn't something most people do overnight. It takes practice and time. Many of the stories you tell yourself are rooted in despair and fear, like Paige's were, and trying to tell yourself a different story might feel a bit like lying at first. After all, how are you supposed to believe "things will get better" when you currently believe "my life sucks and always will"? It can feel like a stretch. Some of the stories you tell yourself may have even taken root in your childhood, stories like "I'm not good enough" or "I need others to make me happy." Overcoming or shifting these may take months! I like to use affirmations or incantations to speed up the process.

Affirmations are words or phrases that you can write or say out loud over and over again as a way to train your brain—and yourself!—to believe them.

By now you should understand how your thoughts and how you talk to yourself influences your emotions and actions. How you speak to yourself also conditions your beliefs, and your beliefs dictate how you show up in the world. Your beliefs are essentially the filter to your reality.

Affirmations help overwrite limiting beliefs with more empowering ones. You don't even need to believe your affirmations at first! When you repeatedly write or say empowering words or phrases to yourself for as few as five minutes a day, you start to rewire your brain, and that's when you'll begin to believe those new beliefs. Why would you want to do this? Because new thoughts equal a better reality!

I encourage you to come up with your own affirmations, but here are some examples to get you started:

"I am forever changed and will never be the same person, but I am okay."

"I am never truly alone. I will use my voice to ask for help."

"I'm growing stronger and stronger every day, and I will find my way."

"I am living the life my spouse would have wanted me to live. I will honor our love, not my loss."

"Slowly but surely, I am making a new life for myself."

"I am 100% in charge of my own happiness."

"Good things are happening."

Incantations are the same thing as affirmations, but they have a little more oomph behind them. For example, take an affirmation like "Good things are happening," add in some physiology and emotion (like a fist pump and excited "YES!" at the end), and you have an incantation.

It doesn't matter if you calmly write down your affirmations in a journal each morning or yell out incantations in the shower for five minutes. Either practice is powerful.

One of my daily affirmations is, "Everything always falls into place for me." I literally repeat this phrase over and over again every day, and there have been a few occasions when I desperately needed to believe it.

One of those times was when the coronavirus pandemic took over the world and the U.S. sent all kids home to learn virtually for the first time in history. As pairs of parents were struggling to balance work and home life, I thought, *How am I supposed to do this on my own, without Tim?*

Fortunately, at the time I had a Mexican au pair whose job was to help me cart my three kids to their various extracurricular activities after school during the week and on Saturdays. She graciously agreed to alter her schedule and help entertain the kids for a period of time each afternoon so that I could get some of my own work done.

I adored my au pair, and the kids loved her, too. After I got done helping Samuel, Emmalyn, and Evan complete their schoolwork each day, my au pair would take them outside or entertain them with arts and crafts projects. Anything to keep them busy so that I could sit down to work!

However, my au pair had booked a trip back home to Mexico for a week to visit her family, and, as the U.S. extended virtual learning a few more weeks, my au pair boarded a flight home. Three days later, the U.S. closed the Mexican border, and she wasn't allowed to return.

Massive overwhelm threatened to cripple me when I got the news. I walked into my garage, hid in a dark corner behind a rarely used outdoor freezer, and began to sob. Not only was I going to have to continue to homeschool three elementary-aged kids every morning, but I would also need to entertain them, feed them, bathe them, and keep them out of my Zoom calls while cooking, cleaning, and doing every other household chore that needed to get done. Almost immediately, I thought, *I can't do this! I'm only one person! I hate my life!*

Now, I realize that I'm not the only person on the planet who had to make drastic adjustments during the pandemic and that it created all kinds of struggles for people all over the globe, but I tell you this story to point out how quickly I fell into a negative thought pattern. And where did those thoughts get me? Nowhere.

It wasn't until I ended my pity party with a silent cry for help and a pleading-like repetition of my affirmation ("Everything always falls into place for me") that I was able to pull back my shoulders, wipe the tears off my face, and walk back into my house to face the day.

I immediately notified the au pair agency about my situation and started entertaining all kinds of options. Then, the very next day, I got a call from the agency about a different Mexican au pair, one who was still in the U.S. and looking for a new host family. For whatever reason, things weren't working out with her current host family, and she was looking to move in with a new family as soon as possible. She was currently living literally thirty minutes away in a nearby town.

I ended up interviewing this new au pair that afternoon, and because she was just as wonderful as my first au pair, she ended up moving in with me that very night. She turned out to be a major blessing during a difficult time.

When I told my mother this story, she immediately said, "Things always fall into place for you, Jen." And it's true. I've trained my brain to believe that things will always fall into place for me, and because I've come to believe it so vehemently, they do. My affirmation has led me to seek out opportunities and take far different steps than I would take if I were following a limiting belief like "My life sucks." That is why affirmations are so powerful!

The way you talk to yourself plays a huge role in how you feel and the actions you take in life. Start paying attention to your thoughts, change your story to something more positive, and use affirmations to overcome limiting beliefs you may be holding on to. When you do this, you'll no doubt feel an emotional shift and you'll no longer feel so stuck. Instead, you'll find yourself taking steps to create a better reality for yourself!

7

KNOW YOUR "WHY"

When's the last time you felt motivated to do something? Maybe you wanted to learn a new hobby or to take on a new challenge at work. If it was more recent, maybe you wanted to sort through your spouse's personal belongings or improve your financial situation now that you're on your own. Whatever that "something" was, a decision sparked inside of you and from there, you took steps to make it happen.

As a widow, I have been motivated to do big things, like selling the house that Tim and I lived in and moving across the United States to surround myself with family, and smaller things, like hiring babysitters to give myself much-needed sanity breaks from my little ones. But to talk about the idea—and importance

—of finding your "why," I'd like to take you back to my pre-widow days, to when Tim and I first entertained the idea of even having our third child.

In my mind, three was the perfect number; however, Tim only wanted two children and, after Emmalyn was born, he couldn't understand why I kept talking about having a third. In Tim's logical engineering brain, he had equated two children to one-on-one defense, which seemed manageable. Having a third would create the need for a "zone" defense, which didn't sound as easy.

Throughout my life, I had been surrounded by friends and family members with two or more siblings, and I always envied the liveliness of their households. I feel inclined to point out that I'm also the oldest of twenty-six grandchildren, and my favorite memories as a child involved getting together with all of them at my grandmother's house on Sunday afternoons and holidays and at birthday parties. To me, the more family that was around, the merrier the occasion.

My desire to have a third child was sparked by my love of big families, and I became hellbent on creating one of my own. So what did I do? I took this burning desire and convinced Tim of how much fun a third child would be, overcoming his every objection—even when he exclaimed in horror, "But we'd have to buy a minivan!" I assured him that we could find a more "hip" vehicle with a third row. In the end, he agreed that having another child around would be fun. He began researching new vehicles, I began preparing another nursery, and together we grew excited for another child to enter our world.

The spark within me to have a third child was rooted in my own upbringing and personal experiences, but often we are driven to do something new or create a change based on our current circumstances. As we grow and evolve, we begin to desire and do different things. Each new undertaking requires motivation. Without that motivation, we'd do nothing.

We all have reasons for doing the things that we do, whether those things are related to our families, our work, or even our health. Those reasons are like little bursts of inspiration that cause us to say, "I want that," "I need to do this," or "I'm going to do that."

Whether you realize it or not, each and every time you begin taking action toward something new or different, you are being led by your "why." Your "why" is your source of internal motivation. It's what lights a fire within you and gives you the push you need to start taking action. Even your decision to pick up this book was based on a "why"! Perhaps you wanted to feel less alone by reading another widow's story, or maybe you wanted to learn what steps you could take to survive your loss. Whatever the case, your reason is why you're now reading this chapter!

Motivation is not something that comes easily during the early stages of grief. If you're anything like I was as a newer widow, then you're likely struggling with motivation to do basic everyday things, like getting out of bed or managing the laundry. It's hard to feel motivated to do much of anything when you're feeling so low! I often talk to widows and widowers who are stuck between despair and anger or guilt, who want more for themselves and their overall lives but catch themselves thinking, *What's the point?*

The point is, you have a lot of life left to live. I know how hard this journey feels in the beginning, but at some point, you have to ask yourself: Do I want to live the rest of my days sustaining a sorrowful life, or do I want to experience joy and happiness again? You can absolutely have the latter. You don't even have to know how you're going to get there; you simply need to dig up the motivation to move in that direction.

Why might you want to move forward, feel better, and have a life worth living?

Maybe you already know the answer to this. Perhaps you want to set a better example for your children or do more to help them thrive. Maybe you want to live a life that honors your spouse, or one that would make them proud. Or maybe you're tired of just existing and want to start living more fully.

Whatever the case, getting to the heart of your

"why" is super important. Knowing why you want to climb out of survival mode and live more fully is one thing, but feeling it on a deeper level is the goal. The latter is where your motivation comes from. When you know your "why" on a surface level, obstacles and self-doubt may cause you to slide backward, but when you know it on the deepest of levels, it will inspire you to action and keep you moving forward even when life feels tough or things don't seem to be going your way.

I'd like to walk you through an exercise that helped me find my "why" when I decided that enough was enough. I wanted to climb out of survival mode and make some changes, but first I had to uncover my deeper motivation for doing so.

I learned this tool from Dean Graziosi and Tony Robbins during the Knowledge Broker Blueprint program. Throughout the course, I learned a slew of excellent tools that aided my personal growth and trajectory in life, but this one specifically helped me to understand my deepest reason for wanting to move forward and create a better life for myself and my kids. And, once I uncovered my "why," it anchored in my soul, replacing all self-doubt. It pushed me forward and motivated me to take action.

This exercise, called 7 Levels Deep, will help you uncover the driving force within you to close the gap from where you are to where you want to be. So take out your notebook or a piece of paper and a pen, and get ready to dig deep!

7 LEVELS DEEP

There are seven "levels" to this exercise, and it will likely take you ten to twenty minutes to complete. To start, write down "Level 1" at the top of your sheet of paper, then "Level 2" under it, then "Level 3," etc., until you get to "Level 7." Be sure to leave a line or two of writing space under each "level."

Once you've done this, I want you to think about what you truly want for yourself now that you're on your own. It might simply be to feel better or to make peace with your situation. I've also had widows and widowers tell me that they want to feel more confident on their own, or that they want to find a way to make their lives matter. There is no wrong answer. When I completed this exercise, I wanted to stop simply surviving life and start living an "extraordinary" one. Whatever your answer, write it down next to "Level 1."

Next to "Level 2," write down this question: "Why is it important to you to _____?" Insert what you truly want for yourself in the blank space, and then answer the question. Continue to do this for the next five levels, answering "Why is it important to you to _____" each time. The first few answers will likely come easily, but as you move from level to level, you'll find yourself slowing down. This is because you'll be forced to get out of your head and into your heart. Your "why" will start to become clearer and clearer, and by Level 7, it will be tugging at the depths of your soul. That's the "why" we're after—the "why" that will propel you forward!

I've listed the answers to my own 7 Levels Deep exercise below.

Level 1: What do you want for yourself going forward? *I want to live an extraordinary life.*

Level 2: Why is it important to you to live an extraordinary life? *Because I want to have a fulfilling and meaningful life.*

Level 3: Why is it important to you to have a fulfilling and meaningful life? *Because I learned firsthand how short life can be, and I want to do more than survive mine.*

Level 4: Why is it important to you to do more than survive your life? *Because my heart is tired of hurting, and I no longer want to struggle.*

Level 5: Why is it important to you to no longer struggle? *Because I want to create a better life for myself and my kids.*

Level 6: Why is it important to you to create a better life for yourself and your kids? *Because we only get this one life, and I want to show my kids and others what's possible.*

Level 7: Why is it important to you to show your kids and others what's possible? *Because we all face chal-*

lenges and tragedies, and I want to prove that it's possible to experience joy in life despite those things.

Note that your answers may look far different from mine, and that's okay. I've seen and heard all kinds of answers for each level, and the "why's" have been just as varied—ranging from "I want to give my kids a good life" to "I *deserve* to be happy!"

Now it's your turn! Take a minute to do this exercise on your own. Again, the first two to three answers may come easily for you. Don't put the exercise down if you find yourself taking a while to answer the questions as you move from level to level. Stay with it, sit with it for a bit if you have to, and see what comes up for you. If you start to get emotional, that's okay! The goal is to dig until your truest reason for wanting to get to a better place or create a better reality for yourself presents itself. You'll know you've got it because it will pull on your heartstrings. And, by the time you get to Level 7, you'll have a heartfelt reason for moving forward.

Once you have your truest "why," give yourself a pat on the back. So many widows and widowers—people in general!—remain stuck in survival mode because they're unmotivated to make any changes. But not you! Now that you have your "why," I want you to put it everywhere! Stick it on sticky notes around your home, turn it into a desktop image on your laptop, have your phone send you reminders of your "why" every morning—you get the idea!

Getting clear on your "why" is the first step to creating positive changes in your life. Now that you've uncovered your motivation, it's time to figure out what might elevate your spirits so that you can take action, or steps, to climb out of survival mode and thrive.

8

HOW TO CREATE A FULL AND HAPPY LIFE ON YOUR OWN

What do you want for yourself? Like, *really* want for yourself?

Have you ever sat down to answer this question? Have you ever gotten still and thought about your future now that you're on your own?

As a newer widow, I was so busy juggling work, parenting, and house upkeep that sitting down to figure out what I actually wanted for myself didn't even cross my mind. What did it matter what I wanted, anyway? It wasn't like I had time for myself or my own aspirations. I was in survival mode, remember?

But if you want to climb out of survival mode, if you want to begin creating a life worth living, then you must get clear on what you want for yourself. Again, as Tony Robbins says, clarity is power. You have to get clear on what you want so that you can take steps in that direction.

So many of the widows and widowers I've spoken to stumble over their words when I ask them what they truly want now that they're on their own. Many respond with, "I don't know." But I also hear, "I want to feel peace" or "I want to be happy again." The problem is that most of them don't know what steps to take to feel at peace or to be happy again. They don't even know what will make them happy now that they're on their own.

This was me too. When I finally accepted my loss and realized that it was up to me to create a happy life for myself and my kids, I had no idea where to start. I knew I needed to make positive changes, but I didn't know what changes would lead to the balanced, peaceful, and happy life that I craved. I was playing a role that I had never played before: a working, head-of-household, solo mom of three. It was all new to me. I didn't know how to pick up the pieces of this new life and create something wonderful out of it. I didn't even recognize myself anymore, much less know what would make me happy.

But I was done moseying, remember? I knew I had to get clear on what would make me happy so that I could begin taking steps in that direction, and that's exactly what I eventually did. I used the exercises that I'm about to share with you to figure out what would bring me joy, and then I began forging a new path forward.

You may not know who you are without your spouse, but I am pretty certain that there was a *you* before there was a *we*. You may not even know what you want to do, be, or have on a granular level, but you probably know what kind of lifestyle you'd like to live or how you wish to feel at a high level (e.g., at peace, happy, enjoying life again). I knew I wanted to feel happy, but I didn't know what would get me there. The exercises and tools that follow helped me with the latter. In doing them, I began to remember desires that were uniquely mine (not Tim's!), ones that had been hidden for years—plus I began to discover some new ones! By taking the time to brainstorm what had brought me joy in the past and what might bring me peace and happiness going forward, I was able to reimagine my future and begin taking steps toward it. These tools will bring you the same clarity so that you can start marching toward better days with not just hope, but also intention. Are you ready?

I used a total of three exercises to gain clarity, and I will share them in the order that I completed them. You do not need to complete them in the same order though! I encourage you to read through all three exercises and then go back and do them in the order that calls to you.

The first (The Clarity Tool) will help you figure out

what might make you happy in the short term. The second (Rocking Chair Visualization) focuses on the long term, or the bigger picture, and the third (50 Desires) will help you fill in all the gaps. I began with The Clarity Tool because I was tired of putting one foot in front of the other and needed immediate direction. I then zoomed out using the Rocking Chair Visualization exercise and determined what I wanted for the rest of my life, and then I used 50 Desires to find ways to make that bigger picture become a reality. You may want to start big and zoom in to the here and now, or use 50 Desires to get your creative juices flowing before diving in to the other two!

If you suddenly feel overwhelmed, then take a deep breath and relax. Don't feel like you have to complete all three exercises at once. If doing one exercise now, one tomorrow, and one the next day feels better to you, then do that! Do not let this process stress you out! These exercises are designed to help you gain the clarity you're lacking right now, and that clarity will help you feel less lost as you begin figuring out the best way to move forward. Just try them, do your best, and know that your best is good enough.

THE CLARITY TOOL

I teach this tool in my course *How to Be Happy + Enjoy Life Again: Strategies for Young Widows + Widowers*, as it's a great first step out of survival mode. It's a tool that I learned in the Knowledge Broker Blueprint program, and it focuses on what you can do in the short term to make sure you aren't in the same place (emotionally or physically) at this time next year.

It's time to pull out your notebook or a piece of paper and a pen! There are four parts to this tool: your current status, one-year goals, why these goals are important, and the capabilities needed to achieve your goals. Ready to get started?

Current Status

At the top of your paper, write "Current Status." This is your reality, or your truth. Under this heading, you'll want to write down what you're feeling or what your life is currently like right now. For example, you might write, "I feel stuck," "I'm not sure who I am anymore," "I'm living day-to-day," "I'm tired of just surviving," "I'm afraid I'll never be happy again," or "I'm worried about my kids." Or you might write, "I want life to feel easier," "I want to help my kids thrive," "I want more time for me," "I want to feel like I have a grip on life," or "I want to feel less lonely." Don't skip this step! All change starts with honesty. You must get clear on where you're at before you can begin to create a better life for yourself.

One-Year Goals

Now fast-forward one year. Pretend you just had the best year of your life. I know this seems like a long shot right now, but I promise you it's not. Remember, your spouse would have wanted you to be happy. You deserve to be happy, and to start moving in that direction, you need to think beyond the present moment. So play along with me for a minute.

You just had the best year of your life. What made it so great? What did you do? What did you see? What did you accomplish? How did you feel?

Think about all of the different areas in your life: your well-being and health, your work and finances, your hobbies and lifestyle, your relationships with your family, friends, and kids, and even your home. What would be different about any and all of these areas if you had just had the best year of your life?

It's likely been a while since you thought about the future in this way. It might even feel really, really hard. One of the widows in my Facebook group, whom I'll call Jane, told me that she couldn't imagine life beyond today because she was living in full-on reaction mode, putting out one fire after another and merely surviving each day. But I encouraged her to pull out her "why" and to give this exercise a fair try. So she did, and in doing so, she said she realized that she would feel more in control if her home were decluttered and organized in the way she wanted it to be instead of the way that her husband had left it before he passed. It would actually feel *freeing!* So this became one of her One-Year Goals.

Others who struggled to start this exercise were able to dream up owning their own homes and contributing to society in new and exciting ways. The possibilities are endless!

I encourage you to sit with these questions for a bit and simply see what comes up for you. Then write it all down and circle the top three to four things on your list that you'd most like to accomplish or change. These will become your goals for the next year. Don't worry about how you'll achieve them. We'll get to that!

Why These Goals Are Important

In the last chapter, we discussed why it's important for you to move forward and create a full and happy life. Here, I'd like you to write down why these three to four specific goals—the ones that will help you create the best year of your life!—are important to you. For example, Jane's goal to declutter her home had everything to do with her desire to regain control of her life. The reasons for your goals may be related to the kind of example you'd like to set for your kids, the quality of life you'd like to have, or the legacy you hope to leave.

Just like before, try to get out of your head and dig

deep. You want to get to the heart of what these goals mean to you. In doing so, you will anchor the goals so that achieving them becomes a must. And when they are a must, you'll find a way to make them happen, causing the best year of your life to come to fruition.

Capabilities Needed to Achieve Your Goals

For the final part of this exercise, think about what knowledge you'll need to acquire, what people you'll need to talk to, or what steps you might need to take in order to begin moving in the direction of your goals. For example, if your spouse used to handle your finances and your goal now is to climb out of debt, then you might add "Budgeting Skills" or "Certified Financial Planner" to your list. If you'd like to live closer to family or buy a house that you can make your own, then "Real Estate Agent" might make your list. If you spent weeks, months, or years taking care of a sick spouse and would like to start taking care of yourself now, then maybe write down "Self-Care." Don't worry about getting too detailed here. In the next chapter, we'll flush these items out some more and turn them into actionable steps toward your overall goals!

How do you feel? You now have a list of One-Year Goals that will help move you in a direction that feels good again. In the next exercise, we'll zoom out and get you thinking about your bigger life desires, which will bring you even more clarity.

ROCKING CHAIR VISUALIZATION

If you're feeling like the entirety of your future is uncertain, then the Rocking Chair Visualization exercise will help. This exercise is one that I learned from Tony Robbins and it's so powerful that I teach it in my course *The Top Five Emotional Challenges Young Widow(er)s Face… and How to Overcome Them*. This exercise not only provides a different perspective regarding your overall life, but it will help you identify big-picture desires that you have for yourself, and these will help provide you with even more direction as you begin to move forward.

To start, go somewhere quiet and eliminate as many distractions as possible. Power down your laptop, put your phone on silent, and shut your door if you must! Then close your eyes and picture yourself sitting in your rocking chair at ninety years old. Maybe you're in your living room or maybe you're on your front porch. Whatever feels peaceful to you will work. As you visualize yourself gently rocking back and forth and reflecting on the long life you've lived, I want you to ask yourself these two questions: "Did I have an extraordinary life or just a mediocre life?" and, "What would make my life an extraordinary one?"

Remember, just because your life didn't turn out the way you expected it to doesn't mean that the rest of your life can't be better than you ever imagined. How your life unfolds from here is up to you! So if you want to figure out what would make your life an extraordinary one, then I encourage you to think about what matters to you. What are you passionate about? What types of things did you enjoy as a child? What activities do you still enjoy? What would you do for work if money weren't an issue? Would you like to travel, learn a new language, have more friends, own your own business, or volunteer more? Don't think about the things that you don't want. You have to step away from those things that you don't want in order to achieve clarity. Instead, think outside the box as if the sky were the limit—because it is!

One of my clients, a widow I'll call Sarah, told me that the first time she closed her eyes to answer these questions, she thought, *I've got nothing!* But she desperately wanted some direction in life and so she tried again, sitting quietly until thoughts began to form. It was then that traveling, helping others, and becoming more healthy and active presented themselves, as did the bigger goal of being able to chase her grandkids around when she's eighty! Being healthy and active comes up for a lot of my clients actually, as does traveling. Another client, who was just eight weeks out from her loss and in the trenches of survival mode, was able to picture herself biking around the south of France and writing a book!

Let your mind wander and see where it goes. Then open your eyes and write down everything that came to you. Let this list be what you're now striving for, even if some of your ideas feel a bit lofty. They may not be possible this year or next, but that doesn't mean that they'll never be possible.

Next, put an asterisk next to the top one or two desires from your list, the ones that you'd like to focus on first. You don't have to have a plan to achieve them. We'll get to that later. For now, pat yourself on the back for uncovering what's important to you. Having that bit of clarity will help you figure out what steps to take as you begin to rebuild your life.

50 DESIRES

If you're having trouble getting started with the above exercises or want to flush out or add detail to your bigger-picture goals as I did, then 50 Desires is for you! This exercise can be found in Nancy Levin's book *Worthy* (a highly recommended read!).

Essentially, you're going to come up with a list of fifty desires that you have for yourself. Why fifty? Because anyone can come up with a list of two or three things they want. Heck, I can tell you right now that I want financial security, good health for me and my kids, and dark chocolate by the truckload. I could even create some goals and take specific action based on these desires in the short and long term, but will that be enough to create the fulfilling, happy life that I desire? Probably not.

I like the 50 Desires exercise because it forces you to expand your mindset a bit and gives you even more ways to move forward toward a life that will feel good again.

So go ahead and take out your notebook or another piece of paper and write the numbers one to fifty down the page. Then get comfortable because you're not supposed to get up from your seat until you are done! Your goal is to write one desire next to each number. Think about the little, big, deep, and even frivolous things you might want today, tomorrow, or any day in the future. These could be anything! Allow yourself to dream and don't worry about how any of it will happen. And, of the fifty, you can have five "altruistic" desires for your loved ones (e.g., your children, your parents, your siblings, etc.), but the bulk of the desires are meant for you. This is your journey from surviving to thriving, not someone else's.

Coming up with fifty desires is no easy feat. At least, it wasn't for me. When I completed this exercise, I was sitting in a Toyota dealership waiting for my minivan to get serviced and struggling to get past desire number five. It had been so long since I had thought about what would truly make my heart happy, and I sat there, rubbing my fingers on my forehead as though trying to activate my brain somehow. But, as I continued to let my brain wander, ideas started to come to me and I began writing furiously until I had come up with fifty desires. Mind you, some of them are out of this world and may never happen, things like owning my own plane or having a live-in personal chef, but the idea is to write down anything and everything that you think would be "cool," regardless of whether you think it's possible.

If you're truly struggling to get started, try answering these questions: "What parts of my life would I like to be different?" "What did I dream about when I was younger?" "What experiences would I like to have on my own or with my loved ones who are still here?"

Once you have your fifty desires, print out your list and put it in a place where you'll see it every day. This is not intended to remind you of what you don't have or to dim your spirits, but rather to remind you of what you want now that you're on your own and to shine a light on where you're going. In fact, place an asterisk next to one or two desires that you'd like to work toward now—ones that will help you create the happiness you're seeking.

Take your top few desires from the 50 Desires list and the Rocking Chair Visualization exercise and combine them with your three goals from The Clarity Tool. These are the things that make you tick. They are what matters to you and what you want for yourself.

Now that you have some clarity, it's time to turn those goals into a plan. Why? Because goals without a plan are just dreams—and you want to climb out of survival mode, find peace, and live a full and happy life on your own, don't you?

9

SMALL STEPS LEAD TO POSITIVE CHANGE

Think of a time when you felt exceptionally happy. This could be a time before you met your spouse or one that happened more recently. Maybe you were recognized at work, or you had a great day with your kids, or you accomplished something that made you proud. How long did that happy feeling last? A few days? A few hours?

About a year and a half after Tim passed, I decided to run the Savannah Half-Marathon. I've been a runner since high school, but I had taken a hiatus during 2014 when my pregnancy, the birth of our third child, and Tim's cancer journey took priority. It wasn't until I began seeking a way to relieve the stress of everyday life after Tim passed that I jumped back into running, squeezing in a few miles on my way home from work every other day or getting my father to babysit at the crack of dawn on a Sunday so that I could head out to a nearby trail.

Running, like any form of exercise, provides multiple mental and physical health benefits, and it became like an addiction for me. I equated running to zoning out or "escaping" my reality and relished the emotional high afterward. Eventually, I started going further and further every time I hit the pavement. When I began logging seven- and eight-mile runs, I decided to sign up for the Savannah Half-Marathon.

Half-marathons were not new to me. I had run several before, even one with Tim, but putting one on the calendar that summer served a purpose. It gave me a goal to work toward and a chance to prove to myself that, underneath my grief, the old me was still there.

That November, I not only finished the race, but I ended up completing it in one hour and forty-five minutes—the fastest I had ever run 13.1 miles. I beat my previous half-marathon time by a whole fifteen minutes! I was so proud of myself that I had my new personal record engraved into the back of my finisher's medal before I even left the finisher's area. I was beyond happy! I told everyone I knew all about my accomplishment and felt like I could do anything. The sky was the limit! I was back to my old self!

And then, two days later, when my emotional high fell flat, I thought, *Now what?*

As humans, we tend to feel good when we are

making progress of any kind. Whether you're improving your athleticism or physical health like I did or simply completing projects around your home, you're making progress, and, as Tony Robbins says, progress equals happiness. That's why so many people, not just widows and widowers, are unhappy when they feel "stuck" or "in a rut." Moving forward, achieving and accomplishing things, and just getting things done —in all areas of life!—provides so much satisfaction! That's why so many of us are continually looking for the next project, goal, or way to move forward. Learning, trying, and doing new things feeds our souls, lifts our spirits, and helps us grow as individuals.

Yet, as widows and widowers, we often get stuck doing the same things over and over again and expecting, or hoping, to suddenly feel better. Not only is this the definition of insanity, but—to quote motivational speaker Mel Robbins—no one is coming to save you. Your journey—your life and your future—is entirely in your hands, and if you want life to look and feel better, you must be willing to do things differently. You must be willing to *take different actions*.

The good news is that you now have a list of goals and desires that, once achieved, will have you experiencing that happy feeling I felt the day I crossed the Savanah Half-Marathon finish line. Heck, the mere act of making progress toward your goals and desires will begin to create an internal shift, which will have you feeling better about life on your own. I see it all the time.

One of my clients, whom I'll call Ann, came to me in a state of total despair, two years out from the loss of her husband. She was going down Alice's rabbit hole daily, feeling hopeless about her life and uncertain about her future. She wanted to feel better, but she didn't know who she was without her husband, and she had no idea how to turn her life around.

After I walked Ann through The Clarity Tool, she began to remember the kinds of activities that had brought her joy years earlier, like traveling internationally and playing music, and she identified a few new desires that she had for herself, like working with kids, losing weight, and making new friends. She took all of these discoveries and created four new One-Year Goals related to her health, hobbies, work, and friendships. We then worked together to identify steps that she could take to bring those goals to fruition.

What happened next was beautiful! As Ann began taking those small steps toward her new goals, she started experiencing a significant internal shift. She found herself going several days at a time without crying, and her attitude toward life went from despair to hope and then optimism in less than six weeks. For the first time since her loss, she was excited about her future and actively taking steps to create it!

You can do this, too! Changing your story, focusing

on the here and now, being grateful for what you still have, knowing your "why," and getting clear about what you want for yourself will help lay the foundation for a happy and fulfilling life. But you must then take action. Taking even small steps toward your goals will lead you to the positive change you desire. And again, progress equals happiness. When you begin to take steps toward the life you want for yourself, you will start to feel your spirits lift.

So, are you ready to make some progress toward a more fulfilling life? Great! I'm about to walk you through the system that I used with Ann and many of my other clients. I also use it myself! Tony Robbins developed it to help anyone take their bigger vision and make it real, and it works!

Take out your notebook or another piece of paper and a pen and have your list of goals and desires close by. We are essentially going to chunk them down into small, actionable steps that can be completed within a short timeframe. Try not to let this overwhelm you. Instead, remember your "why" and all of those things that you want for yourself. Action is what's going to close the gap from where you are to where you want to be, and as you begin taking small steps toward your new goals, you'll start to feel the same positive internal shift that Ann did.

The tool, or system, is called RPM, and no, I'm not referring to your car's engine. "RPM" stands for "Rapid

Planning Method," and it's a system many people from across the globe use daily to align with their overall desires in life.

RPM

A better way to think about this system is to equate the acronym RPM to Results, Purpose, and Massive Action. I'll break these down for you individually.

Results

Your goals from The Clarity Tool and Rocking Chair Visualization exercise were likely broad. For example, most of my clients tell me that they want to be healthier, to travel, or to see their kids thrive. Maybe, like Jane, you want to make changes to your home. Maybe you want to rediscover who you are on your own. Maybe, like Sarah, you want to help others. For RPM to work, you'll need to be more specific. Take each of your One-Year Goals and top desires and ask yourself, *What result am I really after?*

For example, if you want to feel healthier, then what does that mean to you? Does it mean that you want to eat more foods that nourish your body so you have more energy? Or does it mean that you want to lose weight so you can keep up with your kids or your grandkids? If so, how much weight do you want to lose and by when? Eleven pounds in three months, thirty-seven pounds in six months, eighty-two pounds in the next year?

If you want to travel more, then how often do you want to leave town? Do you want to travel locally or internationally? Do you want to go solo, with the friends who have been by your side throughout this journey, or with your children?

If you want to help your kids thrive, then in what way? Do you want to strengthen your relationship with each of them, create new routines and traditions with them, or help them get the emotional support they need?

If you want to work on your home, in what area specifically? Do you need to sort through, pack up, or donate your spouse's clothing, toiletries, knickknacks, and other belongings? Do you want to finish all the house projects that your spouse started? Or do you want to redecorate certain rooms to make them feel like your own?

If you want to rediscover yourself, then how might you do this? Do you want to try new sports or hobbies? Which ones? Do you want spend time alone in nature? Or do you want to explore somewhere new on your own?

If you want to help others, then who? Do you want to work with the elderly, volunteer in soup kitchens, or assist other widows on this path? If you'd like to help others on this journey, then do you want to create a local griefshare group in your community or start a foundation? I know widows who have done both and have found these endeavors extremely rewarding!

The more specific you are, the easier it will be to move in the direction you're seeking. This is because, when your desires are too broad, you often don't know where to start, so you do nothing or very little. But when your desires are specific, you can more easily identify some steps to help you achieve what you're after.

Now write down the word "Results" at the top of your paper and list your new, specific goals and desired outcomes beneath it. You should be very clear about what you want now, and when you know why you want what you want, it will be easy to get (and stay!) motivated to move toward each result. This brings us to purpose.

Purpose

For each result, you will want to write down a purpose. This is your "why." What is the reason you wish to accomplish, achieve, or move toward that result? If you want to rediscover yourself by trying a new hobby, for example, then what is driving you to do so? Do you want to explore a potential new interest, build up a new skill, or simply figure out who you are while trying something new with a group of strangers who have zero expectations of you? If your result is related to a house project your spouse started, then what will completing it do for you? Will the finished project eliminate an eyesore in your home, bring you some closure, or simply give you a meaningful way to remember and honor your spouse?

Remember, your "why" helps you associate emotion with the results you want and the actions you are going to take to get there. It's your source of inspiration and motivation! So dig deep and get into your heart for this part. Why do you want each result? What will it do for you, your kids, or your life? When you know the answer, it will drive you to make it happen. So take a minute and write down your purpose next to each result. Then move on to massive action.

Massive Action

Now that you have a clearer picture of what you want for yourself and a very defined list of desires that will do wonders for your spirit as you begin making progress toward each of them, let's talk about the action part in all of this!

When it comes to taking massive action, you don't want to overwhelm yourself. The idea is to chunk your results down to a few small steps that you can begin taking immediately to move yourself forward. I like to think of it as a staircase. If you picture your results at the top of a staircase, then the steps leading up to the landing are literally the steps you will take to get to the top. For each result on your list, you should come up with three actions you can take to jumpstart your journey to the top of the staircase.

For example, if you want to lose eighty-two pounds in the next year, what three things can you do in the next thirty to sixty days to start your weight-loss journey? Could you eliminate high-calorie beverages from your diet, ensure vegetables make up half of your dinner plate three times per week, or walk a mile with your dog every morning? If you want to strengthen your relationship with your children in an effort to help them thrive, could you arrange to spend one-on-one time with each of them for just ten minutes a day, plan a day trip with them, or surprise them in some way? If you want to take steps to rediscover yourself, could you schedule twenty minutes of alone time per day, sign up for a class related to something you're curious about, or join a club sport just to try something new?

It's important to note that you set the timeline here. I recommend completing your massive action steps within thirty to sixty days, but if that feels overwhelming, try doing ninety or 120 days. Or, if you want to make rapid progress, you can set weekly goals! It's completely up to you. There is no right or wrong here.

As you begin to take action, also recognize what's

working and what's not working. If you do one particular action and see zero results, that doesn't mean that you should change the result that you are after. Never change your goal! You put it there for a reason! You put it there *on purpose*. So instead, try taking a different approach. The idea is to keep taking a variety of steps until you begin seeing the results that you want. And when you start seeing those results, be sure to celebrate. You're no longer waiting around to be saved! You're no longer waiting to feel better! You're actively creating a life you can feel good about! Your spouse would be so proud of you.

You now have a list of specific results that will help bring about the fulfilling and happy life that you want, and you've identified small steps to lead you there. So what steps can you take today? If you're struggling to get started, use your purpose, or your "why," to motivate you. Then, as you celebrate each step on the way to that top landing, you'll naturally keep going. That's because momentum will take over!

Remember, as you begin to make progress, your world will start to look and feel so much better. You will begin to experience more hope and optimism, just like Ann did, as well as so much positive change. So what are you waiting for?

10

BUILD EVEN MORE POSITIVE MOMENTUM

Throughout the course of my widowhood journey, I have read many self-help books. Actually, I have read a ton of them, and they all referred to practices that you can do to feel more focused, calm, centered, grounded, positive, and happy. At first, I thought, *Sounds like a lot of work*, and since life already felt overwhelming, I skipped right past them. Yet every time I picked up a new book, ready for words of wisdom that would transform my whole life in an easier way, there they were—the same practices over and over again! Eventually, I got smart and decided to try them.

Of course, I didn't try them all at once, and some of the practices were ones that I had done in my younger years, way before becoming a widow, so it was just a matter of bringing them back into my life. Others were brand new to me, and so I began trying those one at a time.

As it turns out, there is a reason why every book I had read ranted and raved about the effects of these practices. They work! As I tried them, my internal world began to shift even more, and my outlook on life brightened. This was beyond what I was already feeling as a result of changing my story, creating empowering beliefs, coming up with new goals, and marching toward those goals. Everything I was learning related to boosting my overall holistic well-being, something I had seemingly neglected since my husband's passing. After all, taking care of yourself when you're navigating the highs and lows of grief and trying to survive work, childcare, and household chores on your own can feel next to impossible, right?

I eventually implemented all the practices I'm about to share with you, but you don't have to go all-in like I did. Each of the practices has specific benefits. Follow your intuition and commit to trying the one or two that speak to you first. If none speak to you, then pick one or two that feel the most doable to you right now. See how you feel, and then, when you're ready to try another one or to add an additional practice into your daily routine, go for it!

Please note that these are not magical potions or quick fixes. They won't have you feeling differently, or better, today or even tomorrow, though you will notice some of their benefits somewhat immediately. I can almost guarantee that, if you stick with them for at least a few weeks, you will reap the same boost in well-being that I and millions of people around the world have experienced.

What's more, as you begin to feel that boost in well-being, those bouts of loneliness you're likely feeling will start to dissipate. That's because loneliness is an emotion, just like despair. It's our way of going within and connecting with ourselves when we feel disconnected from everything and everyone outside of us.

Of course you feel alone or lonely. You've just lost the most significant person in your world, the person you connected with on a daily basis. It's even normal to feel sorry for yourself. We *all* do this! However, as you begin to increase your emotional well-being using the practices you're about to learn, you'll find those pity parties happening far less frequently because you'll be doing things that fill your cup and lift your spirits. You'll be learning to connect with yourself in a positive way, and you can't experience a negative emotion like loneliness and feel good at the same time. Your brain doesn't work that way!

So, are you ready to feel less lonely and begin building up even more positive momentum in your life? Great! Let's go!

JOURNALING

Before I jump into the more involved practices, I'd first like to discuss the art of journaling. If you despise writing, please bear with me for just a moment! Journaling does not have to be laborious, and there are actually two huge benefits to be gained from putting pen to paper.

Often, when you are struggling with despair, anger, or even guilt, you feel weighed down both emotionally and physically. There are a lot of practices you can use to lift that weight, and journaling is one of them. It essentially enables you to release pent-up emotions by documenting your worries and struggles in the same way you'd talk about them to a therapist. In writing your thoughts and feelings over and over again, you begin the process of letting them go. It's cheaper than actual therapy, and it doesn't have to take long, either. You can write for as short or as long a time as you'd like!

When I began journaling as a newer widow, I committed to writing just two pages every morning. This is something I did as a new parent when I found myself constantly stressed by the demands of motherhood. I would literally pour my heart and soul onto those two pages—anything and everything that was going on in my head—and then leave it all there on the page. Doing so helped me release some of the negative energy I was so often feeling and enabled me to go about my day in a more productive and positive way.

You don't have to write two whole pages or even journal every morning. You can choose to write for thirty minutes before bed instead, or write only in the moments when you feel overwhelmed. I recently encouraged a young widow to journal every time she felt overcome by a sudden wave of grief. She wound up writing for seven to nine pages at a time and felt better each time she did!

Journaling not only provides a therapeutic outlet, but it also helps you recognize and understand your negative patterns—and we all have negative patterns! Often we don't see them because we're too busy living them. We're "in the weeds," as they like to say. But when you've been journaling for a while, you will have the ability to look back at your entries and see firsthand what you're constantly struggling with and what recurring themes keep coming up for you. This awareness is so powerful! When you can see your patterns at a high level, you can take steps to correct or overcome them. This can play a huge part in creating positive change in your life.

I'll give you an example. A little over a year after Tim passed, after I had been journaling for some time, I went back and began reading some of my morning rants and found that I was consistently complaining about my job. Over and over, I would divulge the reasons I disliked my position. I even wrote that I dreaded walking inside my office building! My job was clearly a huge source of unhappiness for me, and yet I was so wrapped up in the daily grind of life—of going from work to solo parenting and household management and back to work again the next day—that I failed to realize how it was affecting every aspect of my life.

When you're miserable, life feels harder, doesn't it? On most days, everything felt like a chore to me, and my patience with my barely school-aged children was teetering between zero and subzero. It took me rereading passage after passage of frustration and dread in my journal to wake up and do something about it. I didn't want to live an unfulfilling life, and I didn't want my kids to grow up with a mom like that. I needed an exit plan, and because of those journal pages, I made it my mission to create one. In the span of just two months, I not only quit that job, but I spent time spoiling my kids before going to work in a new, very fulfilling role with people I grew to respect and adore. My spirits rose exponentially, and my kids saw a whole new side of me—a happier, calmer, and more patient one!

Journaling is just one practice that will help alleviate the weight of grief and give you new insights, though. Meditation is another.

MEDITATION

When I first learned about meditation, I thought, *Isn't that something hippies used to do?* I admit that I was completely naïve about the practice, and even more skeptical about it. I pictured people sitting cross-legged in upright positions with their eyes closed, looking like they were in some kind of quiet trance, and I thought, *I can't even sit still for five minutes!* I was tempted to skip the practice altogether, but given the hype surrounding its benefits and the fact that every mindfulness author on the planet seems to recommend it, I decided to give it a try. And I'm so glad I did.

As it turns out, sitting quietly and focusing on the present—not the past or the future!—for just ten minutes a day can do wonders for your health. According to Deepak Chopra, one of the leading voices in well-being, meditation is a complete de-stressing of the mind *and* body. I didn't experience the rewards of meditation immediately, but I stuck with it for a few weeks, which is what the experts recommend, and soon, I was hooked. The more I meditated, the more my stress levels came down, the more focused I became throughout each day, and the more emotionally stable I felt overall. Even feelings like fear and loneliness began to dull in their intensity, and the deep sense of relaxation that came after each session became addictive. I have become calmer as a result of meditating, and now that I've been doing it for years, I've found that I get answers in the silence. In a sense, when you meditate you reconnect with yourself and with who you are at your core. I went from being a skeptic to being a huge advocate for this practice!

So what exactly does meditation entail? To be honest, not much. Eckhart Tolle, one of the world's greatest spiritual teachers and a master at meditation, states, "One conscious breath in and out is a meditation." Becoming aware of your breath forces you into the present moment, which Tolle says is the key to all inner transformation. Of course, to get the full benefit of the practice, you'll need to do more than take one breath in and out. You'll want to find a quiet space to sit or lie down, get comfortable and close your eyes, and then attempt to clear your mind of its usual chatter (or the thoughts that typically have you stressed out or anxious) for a finite period of time. There are several ways to do this, but the most common types of meditation I've come across are guided and mindful meditation.

During guided meditation, a skilled narrator will walk you through a breathing exercise, sometimes including a full-body scan or other visualization, but always coming back to the breath. Your job is to relax and follow the narrator's instruction. By focusing on their voice, you will free your mind from the things that typically have you overwhelmed or worried, like work, your children, your finances, or even decisions that you wish your spouse were here to help you make. In essence, you're giving your brain the break it needs, which will help you feel better overall!

During mindful meditation, you focus entirely on your breathing without being guided. You simply direct your awareness to where you notice your breath the most, whether that is in your nose, your chest, or your belly as it rises and falls. Many people will set an alarm for ten minutes and then increase it to twenty, thirty, or sixty minutes as they begin to get the hang of meditating. Ten minutes is a great place to start.

Guided meditation is likely an easier way to ease into this practice, and, because meditation is so good for your health, I'd like you to commit to trying it. Simply download Calm or Headspace, two of the more popular meditation apps, and listen to a ten or twelve-minute daily meditation every morning or every night for the next three weeks. If you do your meditation first thing in the morning like I do, then you might find that you feel more focused and calm throughout your day; however, several widow(er)s in my Facebook group like to meditate right before bed because it relaxes their minds and bodies and helps them sleep better! My suggestion is to try meditation at both times of day and see which works better for you.

As you begin your meditation practice, know that it's not going to come easily. Try to suspend all judgment—of the practice and of yourself!—and don't give up before your three weeks are up. It's normal for your mind to turn to memories of the past, to your to-do list, or even to upcoming plans. You've spent your whole life listening to that "monkey mind." Quieting it will not be instantaneous! Simply notice when your mind has wandered and keep bringing your attention back to the narrator. Even if you have to do this one billion times during your first week or two, keep doing it. Keep sitting down to meditate. You are not only training yourself to stay present and increasing your ability to focus every time you do, but you are also rewiring your brain in the process. In time, you will get the hang of it, and you'll start to feel better and better after each meditation.

VISUALIZATION

A practice that's far easier than meditation—and equally rewarding, though in a much different way—is visualization. While in meditation, you become disciplined in the art of quieting your mind to destress and improve your holistic health, in visualization, you allow your mind to have a bit of fun in an effort to help you attract the things you want for yourself. Peak performers in every imaginable industry and top athletes from all over the world actually use this technique to help them achieve their dreams, and now that you have goals and desires of your own, you can use it, too!

Visualization is the act of closing your eyes and picturing your dreams and your goals as if they've already come true. It's like a mental dress rehearsal for your brain.

Why would you want to do this? I'll tell you!

Your brain doesn't know the difference between daydreaming and reality. So when you visualize having already achieved your goals in a way that feels real, you effectively activate your creative subconscious, meaning that, when you open your eyes and go about your day, your brain begins seeking ways to bring the images you just visualized to life! It will start to bring new information, different strategies, and even objects that you desire into your awareness. Sometimes your mind will even present you with a new idea. Ever have an aha moment or sudden spark of inspiration that winds up bringing you closer to a goal? It's just like that.

Every time you visualize, your brain gets to work finding strategies that will help you achieve your desires. In turn, you build even more internal motivation to take action toward your goals and delight in the progress you're making. It's a win-win!

To visualize, you simply need a quiet space and five minutes of uninterrupted time. It helps if you are completely relaxed, so many people do their visualizations right after waking up, after meditating, or just before bed. As you begin to think about the things you want to be doing in your future, the key is to use all five of your senses. What would it feel like to have already achieved your goals? What do you see, what do you hear, what do you smell? You want to bring your desires to life in your mind and make them as real as you can.

For example, if you'd like to start fresh in a new house, what is the feeling that you get when you walk through the front door? What color are the walls? What does your bedroom look like? If you want to become more active, then picture yourself after you've been walking, doing yoga, or taking hikes in nature for a few months. Revel in the newfound energy you're feeling! Imagine yourself telling a friend how much your new activity level is helping you, as they comment on how good it is to see you smiling again. If, like me, you want to travel more, then picture yourself in one of your dream vacation spots and feel all of the details of being there. One place I'd like to travel to is Alaska, and when I visualize being there, I can feel the chill of the air on my skin and the adrenaline rush I get from mushing across the snow on a dogsled!

You can even take your visualization practice one step further by creating a vision board. Vision boards are like inspiration collages that represent your goals and desires through words and pictures. Because your mind responds so well to visual stimulation, these boards have the same benefit as visualization: they activate your subconscious and act as constant motivation for you to keep taking action toward your goals.

I made a vision board about a year after Tim passed and recently had to create a new one because all of my short-term desires, like getting back into running and having potty-trained kids, had come true! It's fascinating how quickly your world starts to change when you get clear on what you want and then spend time focusing on those desires. You start to move in the direction of newly realized goals and dreams!

Making a vision board is easy. Simply find a bunch of old magazines and begin cutting out pictures and words that represent the lifestyle you wish to have, the material things you'd like to acquire, the places you'd like to go, the things you'd like to do or accomplish, and even the feelings you'd like to experience. If you want to feel more joy, then find pictures that depict people smiling or that elicit the feeling of joy within yourself. If you want to be free from all of the debt you may have collected since your spouse's passing, then cut out images of money or pictures of the activities you'll enjoy when you feel financially abundant. You can even cut out the words "JOY" and "DEBT-FREE."

In my course *How to Be Happy + Enjoy Life Again: Strategies for Young Widows + Widowers*, I have widows and widowers create vision boards, and though they often start out reluctant, it always ends up being a fun project. Some of them even have their kids help them! Peace symbols, happy children, and pictures of beautiful destinations are some of the images they cut out in addition to words like "HEALTHY," "GRATEFUL," and "COURAGEOUS." You may want to find aspirational images related to your faith, self-care, and hobbies you'd like to get back into, or look for words and mantras that you wish to live by!

Once you've gathered a bunch of clippings, you'll want to glue or tape them onto a poster board of any size in a way that's visually appealing to you. Then place your finished vision board where you will see it every day and spend two minutes a day looking at all of the pictures and words. This is where you're headed! Take it in and allow yourself to get excited. Feel everything about your future as though it's already here, and then watch as your brain finds ways to get you there.

A NOTE ABOUT EXERCISE

Though it's not a "practice," per se, I'd be remiss if I didn't mention exercise and all the mental and physical health benefits it provides. The mere act of going for a walk can be enough to change your emotional state, which is tremendously helpful when those waves of grief take over, but it also does so much more!

Did you know that exercise can increase your bone and muscle health, provide relief from stubborn aches and pains, lower your risk for diabetes and high blood pressure, make your skin look healthier and younger, improve your memory, and give you an energy boost? It can also improve your mood. This is because when you exercise, your body releases endorphins (a type of hormone) that evoke positive feelings and help push away negative ones. It's like free therapy!

The Department of Health and Human Services recommends thirty minutes of exercise a day, but if you don't have thirty free minutes to go for a walk or run or to get some other form of cardio in either at the gym or at home, then don't sweat it (no pun intended!). You can actually break the thirty minutes down into five-minute chunks and still get the same benefits. Basically, it doesn't matter how you get it done, so long as you do it!

I heavily promote exercise to those in my Widows & Widowers Seeking Happiness Facebook group and to all of my clients because of how much it has helped me on my own journey. Whether you're six weeks out or six years, exercise can boost your well-being. And it doesn't have to be a chore. There are so many ways to make it fun! One widow took to the outdoors with her kids and found that walking and biking worked wonders for all of them. Another began dancing to YouTube videos and found that this significantly reduced her anxiety!

Exercise is by far one of the best ways to overcome

a trip down Alice's rabbit hole or to increase your energy for the day. Whether you head outside for a quick hike in nature, do a few minutes of yoga, dance around your living room, or take a bike ride with your kids, you'll not only find your thoughts and your mood starting to shift, but you'll also be doing something good for your physical health in the process.

Journaling, meditating, visualizing, creating a vision board, and exercising all helped me to increase my holistic well-being, which played an enormous role in my journey out of survival mode. They have become daily habits and have all played a part in helping me move forward. If you'd like to experience even more positive momentum or make more rapid progress toward a better-feeling life, then I strongly encourage you to try these things. Start by implementing one practice for a few weeks and then another for a few weeks after that, like I did, and, if you don't love a particular practice after giving it a solid shot, then you don't need to keep doing it! There are no rules. You may even find that you like doing one or two practices every day and others just a few times a week or at specific moments, like my client who journals only when those tsunami-like waves of grief threaten to take her down Alice's rabbit hole. Do what works for you, watch how your world begins to change, and see how you feel. I think you will be pleasantly surprised.

11

NO TIME, YOU SAY?

By now, you might be thinking, *This all sounds great in theory, but I don't have time to do any of it!* I totally get it. When I learned about RPM, affirmations, gratitude, and all those other practices, I was working full-time, taking care of a toddler and two preschoolers, and managing an entire home on my own. Free time was nonexistent.

Your situation may not look like mine, but you likely have some time-consuming commitments on your plate. Even so, I'd like to remind you that you can make time for the things that are important to you, and I'm going to show you how.

When I decided that I desperately wanted to climb out of survival mode and feel good about life again, I knew that these practices could potentially help me do that. After all, they had helped millions of people all over the globe lead healthier, happier, and more fulfilling lives, and I was craving all of that. I knew that if I made zero changes, then I would continue to feel lost, stuck, and unhappy in life, and so, equipped with my "why," I became determined to create time to implement all of the tools and practices I was learning.

My kids were all under the age of five at the time I decided this, so staying up later was not an option for me. My days started at the crack of dawn and were a constant blur of activity until my kids were asleep in their beds again. I was—and am to this day—completely exhausted by 9:00 p.m. Completing any kind of mental health exercise at that hour would have been a wasted effort, and probably would have put me to sleep! So instead, I trained myself to get up one hour earlier than my kids and began implementing some of the tools and practices before the sun came up each day. In doing so, I experienced the additional benefits of having a stellar morning routine.

Until this point, I had been waking up to the demands of three children who could do nothing for themselves. I was a working solo mom in full-on reactive mode. From the minute I opened my eyes until the minute my head hit the pillow each night, I was servicing everyone else's needs but my own—at home and at work! But when I began spending the first hour of my day in peace, drinking my coffee, meditating, visualizing, or writing my two pages, I felt like a new person. I suddenly became proactive instead of reactive. When my kids woke up for the day, I was ready for them, and as the benefits of the practices started to kick in, I felt more focused, calm, centered, grounded, positive, and happy. It changed everything for me!

I strongly encourage a good morning routine. Whether your morning starts at 5:30 a.m. or 11:30 a.m., a morning routine not only helps set a positive tone for the day, it ensures that you practice self-care every day, which is extremely important for your overall health. If you wait until later in the day to make time for your emotional and physical well-being, you might not get to it at all. Life happens, right? How many times have you intended to go for a walk or to the gym after work only to be derailed by an unexpected meeting or heavy traffic? Sometimes, it has nothing to do with life and everything to do with a loss of motivation! When you commit to self-care first thing in the morning, however, you ensure that it gets done and you feel better for the rest of the day. Plus, when you start the day with some form of emotional or physical self-care, you're more likely to make healthier choices throughout the day.

I know widows and widowers who do nothing but enjoy the quiet of the morning while sipping their coffee and practicing gratitude before getting ready for the day, and others who like to work out first thing in the morning. Everyone is different and there's no right or wrong routine. My morning routine has even changed over the years, and yours may too. At first, I crammed exercise, gratitude, meditation, visualization, and journaling into the first hour of each day. Sounds crazy, right? But I was tired of feeling unhappy, and I wanted to make rapid progress. Since I couldn't leave my children unattended, I purchased a used treadmill from a friend and began walking a mile every morning at 5:30 a.m. While I walked, I did a mindful meditation, practiced gratitude, and visualized all of my desires—with my eyes open so I didn't fall off the treadmill, of course! I then grabbed a cup of coffee, poured my worries and stress onto the pages of my journal, and plotted out my day, keeping my RPM goals in mind before waking up three very sleepy kids. Doing all of these things created a massive shift in my world, and I started to feel so much more optimistic about life in general.

Now that I'm in an even better place, my routine has evolved. I still drink my coffee in peace, meditating and visualizing before getting everyone up for school, but I now exercise and practice gratitude later in the day and journal only when I need to release tension, stress, or anxiety about something going on in my world.

You may not be an early bird, and my morning routine may have you raising an eyebrow in disbelief right now. The thought of waking up an hour earlier may even have you cringing. That's okay! You may operate better during the day or even at night. The good news is that there are other ways for you to free up time so that you can focus on the practices and activities that will lead you to a better-feeling place and help you continue to take action toward your new goals.

I'd like to introduce you to another tool from the Knowledge Broker Blueprint, one that I used to create time for myself outside of my morning routine. It's called the Not-To-Do List and it essentially helps you determine what you can stop doing, hand off, or delegate in order to free up some additional time for yourself. You'll want to take out your notebook or piece of paper and a pen for this exercise!

NOT-TO-DO LIST

To start, think about all of the things you spend your time doing that don't serve your growth, your income, your faith, your family, or even your future. What kinds of activities or chores do you do every week or on a regular basis? Do you still pay your bills by check and drop them off? Do you try to fix everything in your home on your own instead of hiring help? Do you cook dinner every night of the week?

As a new widow, one thing that I spent hours doing every week was grocery shopping. Every Saturday morning, Samuel had karate at 10:00 a.m. and Emmalyn had art class at 11:00 a.m. I would pick them up after their classes, drive them home, drop them off with Evan and a babysitter, and then head back out to the grocery store. I worked Monday through Friday and didn't have a babysitter on Sundays, so this became my monotonous Saturday routine.

Between the commute to and from the grocery store and the hour it took to shop, I easily spent two hours on this single chore every weekend. That is, until a good friend of mine, who also worked full-time and yet managed to spend her weekends doing fun things with her family, divulged her secret: online grocery shopping. She ordered her groceries online during the week and then spent fifteen minutes picking them up whenever it was convenient for her on the weekend. After hearing this, I immediately began ordering my own groceries online and then picking them up on the way home from Emmalyn's art class every Saturday. This seemingly small change in my schedule freed up nearly two hours of my weekend, which I then used to go for runs, meet up with friends, or take my kids to the park —all things that lifted my spirits and kept me moving forward.

We all do things that take up needless blocks of time, and we often use these things as excuses for not doing the practices and activities that would be good for us or that would help us get to a better-feeling place. But if you can learn to stop, automate, or delegate those chores that have become a "time-suck," like I did with grocery shopping, then you will begin to free up some time for the things that will actually help you move forward. You don't even need huge blocks of time to put the tools and techniques you've learned in this book into practice. You just need little chunks of time here and there, and taking those little chunks of time to focus on these tools and techniques will help get you from where you are to where you wish to be much more quickly than if you did nothing at all.

Take a minute now and write down at least five chores or activities that you typically do in any given week but could stop doing, automate, or hand off entirely. Could a home improvement project that's taking up a ton of time be handed off to the neighborhood handyman? Could you stop taking your kids to and from school every day and instead create a carpool of sorts with a neighbor? If your children are older, could you delegate some chores to them? This is something that I did as soon as my kids reached school age, giving them a nominal allowance for help around the house. At first, it was tough to teach them how to take out the trash, fill the dishwasher, or do their own laundry, but once they mastered those tasks, they felt empowered (and rich!), and I used the small amounts of time I gained back to sneak in a run on my treadmill or to sit down and journal!

As you make your Not-To-Do List, I'd like you to also spend a moment thinking about the people in your life. You obviously can't delegate or hand off people, but you can absolutely limit your interactions with those who hinder your progress forward. Think about those who tend to drain your energy or dampen your spirit whenever you speak with them on the phone or hang out with them in person. Is there anyone in particular who acts as a constant stream of negativity, who only talks about the past and their current problems, or who always seems to frustrate you instead of lifting your spirits? For one of my clients, this was her mother-in-law. A simple text or Facebook post dragging the past into the present or judging her for trying to move forward "too soon" was enough to deflate my client for the rest of the day. For you, your stream of negativity might be a childhood friend, a neighbor, a coworker, or even one of your well-meaning relatives. If so, I'd like you to add those folks to your Not-To-Do List and, if possible, plan to stop interacting with them altogether. If it's not possible to avoid communicating with them—maybe they're a sibling or an in-law, for example—then do your best to reduce the amount of time you spend with them and be sure to set clear boundaries. Doing so may not free up much of your time, depending on how often you're in contact with them, but it is super important to your journey. Who you spend your time with will directly influence your ability to climb out of survival mode and thrive.

Famous entrepreneur, author, and motivational speaker Jim Rohn once said, "You're the average of the five people you spend the most time with." This is because we are social creatures, and, as such, we tend to pick up on the habits, behaviors, and attitudes of those around us. So when you talk to someone who's a ball of negative energy or who has lower standards than you care to have for yourself, you become a little like them, whether you wish to or not. When you're around negative people, you begin to highlight your problems the same way that they do and essentially live life to their standards instead of focusing on the positive or on opportunities. Have you ever noticed how, after speaking to someone who drains you, you feel less positive and less motivated to take action in your own life? On the other hand, after speaking with someone who's got a cheery demeanor and is living life in a way that you find admirable, you tend to feel inspired. You actually want to live up to their standards and become a better version of yourself!

If you truly wish to climb out of survival mode, it will become increasingly important for you to limit your time with those who hold you back and unknowingly prevent you from moving forward toward a healthier, happier life. Instead you will want to surround yourself with positive dreamers and doers who encourage you and believe in you, even when you don't believe in yourself. These are the people who will highlight your strengths because they want to see you succeed, and they'll pull you forward as you begin to rebuild your life. Regardless of whether they're your family members, colleagues, childhood friends, or new acquaintances, they will be your spirit-lifters and will become increasingly important to your journey forward.

Once you've added the negative people in your life to your Not-To-Do List, pat yourself on the back! You've just found a handful of ways to create space in your life for the things that will move you forward! The next step is to implement some of them. Which items on your list can you commit to doing this week? Remember, positive change won't happen if you don't free up space to create it, so why wait? In fact, once you've decided on the best ways to get back some bits of time, think about all of those mental health practices and physical activities you learned about in the last chapter and pick one that you'd like to try in the free time you've just uncovered. Would you like to reap the benefits of meditation, attract new desires into your life through visualization, or destress through journaling? Might one help you move closer to one of your goals— like, might walking every day move you closer to the physical health you desire? Which one could you possibly add into your weekly routine?

I hope you now see how you can make time for the things that will move you forward. Knowing this and taking action are two different things, though. If you find yourself struggling with motivation to create a morning routine or to make changes in your schedule in an effort to free up time during the week, then I encourage you to go back to your "why." Remember your reason for wanting to feel better and to experience a more fulfilling or enjoyable life, and take a look at the goals and the desires that you have for yourself. You deserve each and every one of them, and your spouse would be so proud of you for doing such wonderful things with your life. But these goals and desires will not suddenly appear as your reality and you will not feel less stressed and anxious, more focused, and more at peace if you don't create time to work on your holistic health and take action toward the life you desire.

I know that rebuilding a life in the middle of your life is not easy to do, but it is doable—and I've done it. Make the time, give yourself the gift of holistic health and well-being, and start taking steps forward. When you do, your world will begin to look far brighter than it does today.

12

GIVE YOURSELF SOME GRACE

You now know a variety of techniques that will help you to feel relief from your grief, you've identified new goals that feel exciting, and you've learned practices that you can use daily to build some positive momentum in your life. Exciting, right? But you might be asking yourself, *Will doing these things make the highs and lows I keep experiencing finally come to an end?*

Unfortunately, no. You will definitely begin to experience more good days than bad, and the tsunami-like waves of grief will lessen in frequency and intensity, but they may never fully go away. That's because you will always have triggers. We all do, and they are different for each of us. For you, hearing certain song lyrics on the radio or innocent strangers inquiring about the whereabouts of your spouse may cause you to well up with tears. For me, it's often a moment of overwhelm. An unexpected bill, constant fighting between my kids, or a sudden broken household appliance will have me longing for Tim and the days when he'd swoop in with reassurance, a solution, and the ability to make everything right in my world.

At the time of this writing, I am six years out from my loss and menial things still trigger my grief. Only now, I know how to quickly dissipate the negative emotion before I head down Alice's rabbit hole. I'll give you an example. Recently, the top of my favorite water bottle landed perfectly in my kitchen sink garbage disposal and I couldn't get it out, no matter how hard I tried. Immediately, Samuel offered to use his "smaller hands" to reach in and grab it, but the bottle top filled the hole perfectly, with little room to spare. As Emmalyn and Evan began offering up words of encouragement, I tried everything, from sticking utensils down the grimy hole to lifting the sucker out using wooden toaster tongs, but it was to no avail. The darn thing wasn't coming out.

Seems trivial, right? But it was enough to make me bow my head over the kitchen sink in frustration and despair. I couldn't help but think about how Tim would have been there in a flash with a crafty idea to get the cap out of the garbage disposal. As I began to ruminate over how seemingly difficult life was in these challenging moments without him, I could feel myself starting to go down Alice's rabbit hole. But then Emmalyn quietly asked, "Do you wish Daddy were here?" My heart hurt for all of us at that moment, and I knew I had to change my story. I had to make the transition from "life is hard" to "I can do hard things." After all, I was my kids' role model, the captain of our ship, and I needed to show them that we could figure anything out!

Seconds later, I turned on the garbage disposal, not really sure what I was doing. But it worked! The disposal cut small ridges into the rim of the top, enabling me to latch my fingernails into one of the new grooves and pull the top out of the sink. Emmalyn and Evan quickly jumped for joy, yelling, "Mommy, you did it!" and Samuel, in a very calm and matter-of-fact way, told them, "That's because she never gave up." It's a message I've tried to instill in my kids since they were small and one that I have to remind myself of often.

The incident was so small in the grand scheme of things, but the stuck water bottle cap was enough to trigger my grief nonetheless. I could have easily continued down Alice's rabbit hole, spending the rest of the day feeling hopeless and helpless and taking it out on the kids by sulking and refusing to play. Instead, I changed my story and, ultimately, the outcome of our entire day. I was so proud that every one of my kids had jumped in to help me with either physical or emotional support and that everyone had learned firsthand the importance of never giving up that I decided to take them all out for ice cream cones! I celebrate the smallest of victories to this very day, and I encourage you to do so, too.

We *all* get triggered, even those who aren't widowed. As Tamara Levitt, the Canadian author and voice-over narrator on the Calm meditation app, explains, the key is learning to become aware of your reactions so that you can begin to create healthier ones. Rather than going down Alice's rabbit hole or turning to food and alcohol to momentarily dull frustration, pain, or sadness, you can change your story as I did or simply learn to become comfortable in the discomfort. Allow yourself to feel your emotions without letting them take you down, and instead let them pass through you. The waves of grief will always retreat, and in the process of learning to change your reactions, you will grow. As Levitt states, it is in this way that difficulty or hardship begins to transform you—in a good way!

Going forward, you have a choice to make every single day and in every single moment. You can choose to focus on the past, getting triggered left and right and staying stuck there, or you can choose to be grateful for the time you had with your spouse while taking steps, like changing your story, in an effort to turn your life around. Remember, survival mode is not meant to be a place to stay. It doesn't matter what your family thinks, or what your in-laws, your best friend, your neighbors, or even the cashier at the grocery store believes about the grieving process and whether you choose to move on. They are not in your shoes. You are the author of your life story, and you alone have the power to make it a good one. You alone have the power to regain control over your life and to make your days count.

With that said, climbing out of survival mode does not happen overnight. Setbacks and triggers will continue to pull you back down until you learn to manage your reactions to them. Keep practicing the techniques I shared on how to shift your thoughts and the stories you tell yourself and use those techniques to feel relief in hard moments. In time, you'll be able to turn a moment around as quickly as I did when my garbage disposal threatened to eat my water bottle top!

That's not to say that, once you master these techniques, your journey will be smooth sailing or that there won't be other obstacles on your path. Many of the widows and widowers I speak with suffer from self-doubt and, now that you're on your own, you may struggle with this, too. It's totally understandable! Making decisions related to your home, your career, and even your kids without the input and validation that you're used to receiving from your spouse can feel scary! But I promise you are capable of making good decisions on your own. You simply need to build up your self-confidence.

In fact, pull out that notebook or piece of paper and

a pen and we'll overcome that roadblock right now! I'd like you to make a list of everything you've done since your spouse passed. Yes, everything! Chances are the list will be long. You likely had to pick out a funeral plot for the first time, learn how to manage a home on your own, do things that your spouse used to do, or find ways to connect with your children in a way that you didn't have to before. If it hasn't been that long since your spouse passed, then take a look back on your entire life, at all of the choices you have made and the activities you've completed on your own. Did you graduate from high school or earn a university degree? Did you interview for a job and get it? Did you set an intention to learn a new language, a new hobby, or a new skill and then master it? What are your strengths and what have they helped you accomplish?

If you're struggling to come up with "significant" things, then I want to remind you that even seemingly little things likely felt monumental to you at first and should therefore be added to your list. One of the widows in my Facebook group listed grocery shopping and starting to cook again after the loss of her husband. Later, she added comforting her grieving kids, snow blowing her driveway, and driving her oldest daughter hours away to college all by herself. All of these tasks felt insurmountable before she began them, and yet she did them. As she added up all of the little and big things she had done and was continuing to do, her confidence in her ability to handle life on her own began to rise.

When you're done making your list, I want you to take it and place it where you will see it often. Use it to remind yourself of all that you've done up until now and let it give you a confidence boost whenever self-doubt begins to creep in. You can even add to the list as you begin accomplishing more and more on your own, which you will no doubt do. In time, your self-doubt will begin to fade and a newfound self-confidence will replace it.

Worry, or stress, may also threaten to keep you stuck or prevent you from moving forward. That's because, when you're feeling overwhelmed, you often take minimal action, if any at all. You start to feel like certain things are out of your control and you don't know how to tackle the things seemingly within your control, and so you do nothing.

Both worry and stress often stem from fear of not knowing what an outcome will be, and this will keep you rooted to the spot instead of taking uncertain action. But taking zero action will not move you forward! If you can push past fear, there is often a bit of joy and happiness on the other side. Isn't that what you want? So how do you build up those courageous muscles and take measures to overcome "what if"s or situations that seem out of your control? Turn to a blank page in your notebook or take out a new piece of paper—I'll walk you through another exercise that will help you do just that.

First, it's helpful to get really clear on what's causing your fear. Take a minute and write down all of the things contributing to your stress right now. Are you worried about what's going to happen to you or your kids? Are you distraught over work or lack of work? Are you anxious about your finances? Are you feeling overwhelmed because there are so many things you know you need to do but you can't find the motivation to do them?

Next, we're going to create a plan. Remember, progress equals happiness… and how do you make progress? With an action plan!

Turn your piece of paper over and write down the following three category names: "I Can Control," "I Can Influence," and "Everything Else." Under "I Can Control," I want you to list all the things that you have complete control over that are contributing to your fear or worry. These are tasks or activities that you can complete on your own without help from anyone else. I've had widows and widowers list tasks like "take control of my health" and "improve my financial situation" here. Under "I Can Influence," I want you to write down all the things on your list that you can partly resolve on your own, or at least influence the outcome of through your behavior or actions. Here, I've had widows and widowers list "improve relations with my kids" and "update my will." Finally, take the rest of your list and put it under the category of "Everything Else." These are things whose outcome won't be affected, no matter what you say or do. Most of the lists I see under this category relate to other people's opinions and actions, none of which we can control!

Once you have divided all the things currently worrying you or stressing you out into the three categories, I want you to do a few things. First, strike through all the items you listed under "Everything Else." There is no sense in spending energy on the things that you can't control or influence, so let them go. You might even want to tear up that part of the paper, set it on fire, or flush it down the toilet. Seriously. There's something freeing in the act of physically letting something go. Second, look at the items that you have partial control over and write down an action that you can take for each one in the next few days. These do not have to be big actions. They can be as simple as making a phone call you've been putting off or doing some research that will help you figure out what you need to do next. Even small steps will begin to turn the tides for you. Do the same thing for the items under "I Can Control," but pick one action that you can take *today*. Then pick another action that you can take tomorrow and the next day, and so on! Not only will your stress level start to go down, but you'll begin creating positive outcomes as a result.

I encourage you to use this exercise whenever you are feeling overwhelmed, as it will force you to get to the root of your worry and stress, help you identify where you have control, and motivate you to take small steps in the right direction. This is different from RPM, by the way, which is the plan you'll want to follow to move closer and closer to your big-picture goals or desires. In both cases, you will begin to close the gap between where you are and where you wish to be, simply by taking continued action.

As you take this action, think back to your "why," or your reason for wanting to move forward, to feel better, and to have a life worth living. Keep it front and center and let it be your driving force! Remember to stick your "why" on your bathroom mirror, your refrigerator, or on your desk at work, and let it help pull you forward.

Know that there will be entire days when you feel stuck or low. When you're having an off day, give yourself some grace. You're human. No one's journey is perfect. Try changing your story or get outside in nature if you'd like to change your emotional state and feel some relief. Or allow yourself to feel it all and then try to let it go instead of wallowing. You're walking a path that you never imagined you'd be on, and you're doing the best you can every single day. You're not always going to be up. You're going to feel down. The fact that you have the desire to want more for yourself and that you even picked up a book like this speaks volumes about who you are as a person. Appreciate how far you've come and show yourself some compassion. Then pick yourself up and keep going.

As you go, remember to take time for self-care. I cannot stress enough how important this is! Rediscover what speaks to your soul and do more of what lifts your spirits. Also use gratitude, affirmations, journaling, meditation, visualization, and exercise to boost your mental and physical health and to increase your ability to overcome the emotional challenges that are sure to arise throughout your journey. If you want to experience more good days than bad, then this is a must. You can make faster progress toward overall well-being by committing to a few of these practices every single day. They don't take long, and you will be surprised at how quickly your internal and external world will begin to shift. Combine this with the grief relief techniques, self-care practices, and RPM, and soon you'll be making rapid progress toward the more fulfilling, happy life you deserve.

13

THIS IS YOUR COMEBACK STORY

ecently, I was coaching a young widower who was two years out from his loss and still suffering from the emotional roller-coaster of grief. I'll call him James. One minute, James would feel full of gratitude for a heartfelt moment with his teenage son, and the next he'd feel sucker-punched by life over an old photograph or a memory of his wife. This was happening on a daily basis.

When I asked James what his late wife would have wanted for him or what she might say to him if she could communicate with him in that moment, he replied without hesitation, "Go be happy."

You know that your spouse would likely want the same for you. They'd certainly not want you to crumble under the weight of despair or merely survive the rest of your days, constantly suffering from emotional highs and lows due to their departure from this world. They'd want you to carry on with gratitude for the memories you got to share with them and to take the best parts of them, or what you learned from them, with you as you make the most of the days you have left. In other words, they'd want you to do more than exist! After all, you still get to be here.

The majority of the widows and widowers I talk to get this, but they don't know how to climb out of survival mode and make their way to happy. I didn't know how to move forward at first, either. I didn't know who I was anymore or what I wanted for myself, and I feared that my best days were behind me. I questioned everything in my life, right down to my purpose for being here (other than to take care of my children).

But I've come to learn that, no matter who or what we believe in—God, the Universe, Source Energy—our purpose is to find joy in life, despite its ups and downs. No one's life is perfect. There is tragedy all over the world, and we all face individual hardships, both big and small. With each trial, though, you must choose how you respond and what you'll do next.

Your loss was absolutely devastating. No one will argue that. But how you maneuver through your grief and live the rest of your days is up to you. You can choose to do very little and linger forever in despair, or you can figure out how to move forward, thus adjusting, evolving, and healing as you work to bring both peace and happiness back into your life. A young widow in my Facebook group put it perfectly when she said, "You can either be a victim in life, or a victor." Which will you choose?

It wasn't until that moment at Hartsfield-Jackson Atlanta International Airport, when my curiosity about the afterlife was piqued and my mind was opened, that I became determined to be a victor. I made the decision to do more than survive my loss and consciously embarked on a journey that would ultimately transform my entire life. I began seeking answers, strategies, and a path forward in a completely new way, and, as a result, I began to create a life that was even better than I could have imagined. I changed my story, turned my longing for the past into an appreciation for what I had, and rediscovered gratitude for everything I still had in the present. I mastered how to regain control of my emotions when triggers threatened to take me down Alice's rabbit hole, began doing things to lift my spirits every day, and established new daily habits to boost my holistic health so that I could keep all of the positive momentum going. I then created a new vision for myself and began taking massive action in an effort to make that vision my reality. All of these things helped me to do more than just accept my loss. They helped me to grow as a person and to rebuild a life that I'm genuinely proud of, one in which my kids and I are truly happy, one that Tim would have wanted for us.

In fact, as I navigated my own transformation, two of my kids were doing the same. Remember the little boy who was disengaging from his peers, crawling under desks, and chewing on everything in kindergarten? He was actually diagnosed with high-functioning autism and ADHD at the end of first grade and, after I switched him from play therapy to ABA therapy, he did a complete turnaround. Today, Samuel is excelling academically, running 5k races with me, leading classes as a black belt in tae kwon do, and making friends everywhere he goes. His journey was a roller coaster of a ride, but he has accepted that life will never be the way it was in the beginning and now he is making the most of the present moment with a genuine smile on his face (and a proud momma at his back!).

Emmalyn, the little girl who was throwing chairs across her classroom and tearing through her school in a fit of rage, came out the other side of her grief months after I enrolled her in play therapy. I'll never forget the day when her play therapist walked her out to the main lobby where I sat with Evan and announced that she no longer needed therapy. He said that she was consistently drawing pictures of rainbows and smiley faces and that her demeanor was both calm and pleasant, indicating all was right with her world. I asked, "So that's it? We're done? She doesn't need to come back?" Nope! She didn't. Even her kindergarten teacher had nothing but good things to share. Sitting through her first parent-teacher conference, I found myself waiting for a list of anger-related incidents that never came. Instead, I heard stories of a sweet, often chatty Emmalyn who was a delight to have in class. My little girl had found her happy place, and hearing this made my heart dance inside.

While Evan, my baby, never got to experience life with Tim and thus never suffered the way Samuel, Emmalyn, and I did, I've come to believe that he served a great purpose by being here as we struggled through those early days of grief. When our little family was seemingly falling apart at the seams, Evan's innocent smile would always lift our spirits. He was the calm amidst our storm. I used to wonder, *If I had known our fate, would I have had a third child?* But I know now that Evan was born to help us survive our loss. To this day, he is my "angel baby," the child whose sweet face and good nature helped pulled our little family through many dark days.

You, too, serve a purpose and are capable of making a transformation of your own, no matter how old you are or what your individual circumstances may be. Happiness is not an elusive dream or something that you once had and can't get back. It comes from within, and if your desire is big enough, you can absolutely take steps to attain it.

You now know all of the techniques, exercises, and

practices I used to make the journey from surviving to thriving—tools that took me half a decade to acquire and that I still use to this day! Use them as a how-to guide to get unstuck and to begin building a better life for you and your family. Your spouse would want you to!

Remember, moving forward doesn't mean moving on. You can 100% be happy while keeping the cherished memories of your spouse close to your heart. It's not an either/or situation. I still have pictures of Tim sitting on shelves throughout my house, and it's been over six years! As you take steps to increase your mental and physical health and start making progress toward your new desires, those photographs, the song lyrics, and every other trigger that currently causes you to dip into an emotional low won't have the same effect on you. That's because, as you begin to make your way to a better place, you'll start to remember your spouse with fondness instead of sadness, or appreciation instead of longing. You'll actually feel like you have a grip on life again!

One of the first times I felt this way was almost two years ago, when Emmalyn was invited to a playdate with a new friend, which meant that I got to meet a new mom. In my early days as a widow, the thought of having to converse with a happy mom who likely had a happy husband and a perfect life (*do you notice my resentments?*) would have made me cringe and maybe even bail. But this was after I had spent all of that time focused on personal development, and so I packed all three kids in my minivan and headed out to the playdate.

As our girls played together on the playground, my boys engrossed in a game of tag, I listened attentively as the mom talked all about her husband—how handy he was at home, how he helped make important decisions, and how he made family time a priority. Not once did she ask me about my husband, for which I was actually grateful. Dropping the "w" word on an unsuspecting stranger can quickly make things awkward. Most people are shocked to hear it come from someone so young, causing them to fumble over their words or shrug it off like you said nothing at all. Some even make up a sudden excuse to leave the conversation entirely! But I digress.

In my earlier years as a widow, the mom's repeated praise for her husband would have knocked the wind out of my sails. Not only would I have cut the playdate short, coming up with an excuse to leave, but I would have spent the rest of the day sulking over all I had lost, becoming short-tempered with my kids and tossing any ounce of productivity out the window.

That day, though, as Emmalyn bonded with her new friend, the mom had no clue that she was talking to a widow because I had my act together. I had a genuine smile on my face, and, as my three children played happily on the playground, I thought, *I may not be rocking this life* with *my husband anymore, but I'm most certainly rocking it* for *him.*

You can do the same. No matter where you are on your journey, whether you're in the early stages of grief or have been forging a new path for some time, know that you can get to a good place again. You may be doing more than your peers could ever imagine doing on their own right now, and you probably feel like you're drowning most days, but you are resilient, strong, and absolutely capable of getting through this.

That's not to say that you won't ever regress or face obstacles as you try to move forward. You will have moments, even days, where you feel exceptionally over-whelmed, filled to the brim with self-doubt, too apathetic to accomplish a single chore, increasingly uncertain about the future, and lonelier than ever. You may even face challenges at work, with your children, and with your friends or relatives at times. Whatever the case, don't give up! Keep coming back to the tools in this book. Repeat them as many times as you need to get back on track, and, if you want additional guid-ance on how to achieve greater balance, fulfillment, or enjoyment in life, I'm here.

I have made it my mission to help others behind me on this journey—not because I know how difficult it is, though that's part of it, but because I want you to have a great "comeback story" too. I created the Widows &

Widowers Seeking Happiness Facebook group to inspire widows and widowers just like you and to provide a place where finding joy after loss is not just hoped for, it is encouraged. In fact, I invite you to join the group for a daily dose of positivity and the support of more than one thousand young widows and widowers who want to see you succeed on this journey!

I also created courses on how to overcome some of the most challenging emotions you're likely feeling, like fear and loneliness, and to share strategies for living a fulfilling life on your own. My hope is that these resources, which can be found on my website, help you accelerate your journey from surviving to thriving, so that you begin enjoying life again as quickly as possible.

With that said, you don't have to do it all on your own. When the coronavirus brought my twenty-year career as an event manager to a screeching halt, I decided to leave the corporate world altogether and to focus all of my attention on serving those behind me on this path.

At the time, I had a life coach helping me determine the best ways to deliver all of the tips and advice I had regarding the widowhood journey. She's actually the person who encouraged me to launch my Facebook group, create my signature course, and write this book! She has been a tremendous resource for me, often giving me new strategies, insights, and pep talks as needed—*all of the things that I wanted to provide to you.*

And so I decided to enroll in the Robbins-Madanes Training Center, Tony Robbins' official school for life coaching, and become a certified life coach with a specialization in helping widows and widowers just like you.

Throughout my training, I learned all about human needs psychology and mastered the same strategic intervention techniques and methodologies that coaches use to transform lives all over the world. I now spend my days infusing these strategies with personal stories from my own journey as I help beautiful souls like you weather milestone occasions, angelversaries, and daily challenges. I help build up their confidence, empower them to overcome limiting beliefs, and give them the tools they need to rebuild a life that feels good again. If you feel you could benefit from this kind of guidance, then I'd be honored to pull you forward in the same way.

Nothing fulfills me more than giving back to this community. I love watching my clients become healthier and happier and hearing the excitement in their voices as they begin making progress toward new goals, because I've been there. I know what it feels like. After all, I wasn't always this positive. Six years ago, I was lost, depressed, and scared, just like you. But I know that, with a bit of intentionality, you can find your way forward and move toward greater enjoyment in all areas of your life, including health, wealth, career, and even relationships—because I've done it myself.

As you put this book down and return to work, parenting, and all the activities that make up your current reality, remember everything you've just learned in these pages. You can make the journey from surviving to thriving, as I did. You have what it takes—*I am certain of this*. Start by taking action and purposefully doing things to boost your overall well-being, and know that where you're headed—where you will no doubt find yourself in just a few weeks or months of using the tools, techniques, and practices in this book —will be worth your every effort.

You are a beautiful soul who deserves happiness, and my wish for you is that you experience peace in your heart and joy in your life again. It's time for your comeback story. Make this your turning point—the moment you pick yourself up, dust yourself off, and begin to rebuild a life worth living.

Jen Santaniello is a mom, a running enthusiast, a travel fiend, and a bit of a perfectionist. She is also a widow.

When her husband died of cancer in 2014, Jen's whole world was upended. She was thirty-six years old, working full-time, raising three kids all under the age of four, and managing an entire household on her own. She was devastated. Exhausted. Overwhelmed. Angry that this was now her life. And resentful of everyone who still had a spouse and an intact family.

Fast-forward to present day, and Jen is now thriving. She went from barely surviving and feeling like a crazy person to finding balance, peace in her heart, and joy in her life—and she did so using a variety of tools and strategies that she learned along the way.

Jen has since become a certified life coach through the Robbins-Madanes Training Center and offers both courses and coaching to help others achieve happiness while rebuilding lives that they can feel excited about. She believes that all widows and widowers can find their way forward with the right guidance and encouragement.

Jen now lives in Cumming, Georgia, with her three kids, Samuel, Emmalyn, and Evan.

THANK YOU!

Thank you for reading my book! If you're ready to embark upon your comeback journey and want some personalized, one-on-one guidance and support, then let's chat about how I can best serve you! Head to https://jensantaniello.com/coaching/ to schedule a *free* coaching consultation call.

Made in the USA
Columbia, SC
13 January 2022

54213647R00093